Aspects of My Life

Aspects of My Life

Audrey Singh

Library of Congress Control Number: 2019901089

ISBN:	Hardcover	978-1-7960-1325-2
	Softcover	978-1-7960-1326-9
	eBook	978-1-7960-1327-6

Print information available on the last page.

Rev. date: 02/13/2019

To order additional copies of this book, contact:
Xlibris
1-888-795-4274
www.Xlibris.com
Orders@Xlibris.com
790907

Contents

PART I

Relative to...

My lovely husband,
once shorn of his more than waist-length hair,
never grew it again below his shoulders.
His youthful lissomeness was replaced by
a brave but shambling gait of post-paralysis.
But the twinkle in his roving eye
never diminished.

My husband was taken into the Lucknow military hospital
after a car accident left him unconscious, skull damaged,
and semi-paralysed in his seat next to the driver who
had skidded on dust turned to mud by the first rain after
a long dry season.
My air-force brother-in-law was said to have waved his pistol
at an on-coming vehicle because he could not get any to stop
out of simple compassion.
Months later, post-surgery, we had to rescue the patient since
a tender doctor had responded to his boy-like pleadings for a
reduction of his painful anti-biotic injections. Infection spread
into the frontal bones. Only a more resolute civilian surgeon,
removing the diseased skull portion, countered such pleas with
stern promises to increase the number of needles if the patient
protested the administration. No more complaints were offered.
He came home infection-free soon after.

My sister was a fighter, but at her own last battle
she did not get a chance, sedated to aid her recovery
from pneumonia. She didn't want the intervention,
was scared of it.

As we lingered over farewells in Intensive Care,
she begged a cup of tea. The staff hedged; said that
with the probable imminence of sedation, intake by
mouth was not possible. Her eyes pleaded. I backed
up the staff.
That was the last time we were able to speak to each other.

My sister looked like a beached whale as she rode, face-down,
the water-bed.
Her swollen body was tossed rhythmically by the innovation
brought in to save her life when hope was being lost.
She died anyway - but not until her daughter, summoned,
flew in from far New Zealand.
Distraught, she disallowed the proffered post-mortem.
That we still regret.

My grandmother disdained hospitals. She said they were places only for dying: *if you went in you would not come out alive*. We thought it due to the times she grew up in.
In the 1950's, as a student nurse, I knew them to be good safe places, everyone playing their part, doing their bit, under the stern eagle eye of Sister; no first names, restricted visiting, but run with efficiency, compassion and cleanliness, by a hierarchical team of workers, ruled firmly by Matron.

I had never before been present at the moment of death.
I held my mother in my arms and watched her retreating,
receding far off - to where? I only know she had a look
of peace before the light went out.
But she left a turmoil here in me. I may have held her,
but for long she had not spoken. My last words towards her
were of anger and frustration. Was that why she let go?
I heard some months later that, from her semi-comatose state,
she had spoken to my brother; words that grated hardly
and painfully, as though they came by effort of will only.
To avoid quarrels between my sister and me, he said,
she left her photo albums in his care. And her life that we
looked at over and over, he now keeps in his attic.

My husband missed a career in the merchant navy because,
suffering the most common form of colour blindness, he
could not distinguish red from green, port from starboard.
This had little impact on my perception of him until,
upon an ornamental bridge overlooking a lovely lake,
Look at that gorgeous pink waterlily, I said.
And he said, *Where*?

When he came to England to take up an apprenticeship in pottery with Bernard Leach, my husband was only 19. A prospective bride had been selected for him, and it was wished for him to marry before he left India to secure him within the family. But the girl, only 17, said she was not ready.

He sowed his wild oats and made his escape from our shores; but I was on the ship carrying him home.

The poet's death was in the papers. I saw him in a Soho pub
aeons ago. He looked at me in my sari and lurched across
and stood; but I could not understand his mumbled question
and, pissed, he could not hear my reply. My companion said,
that's Dom Moraes. It meant nothing. That he was from India
impacted more.
We met again years later, when he brought to our house his
mousy English bride. He'd come to see my father-in-law -
well known for his pottery and Punjabi philosophy. I never said,
I met you in a Soho bar. And he didn't even notice me at all.

At table one day, my husband's sister said of her son,
just beginning his medical studies in Dublin, *My boy
won't present me with an Irish colleen for a wife.*
Was it just thoughtless? or was it a personal dig at me?
There was mention of his maybe going on for further
studies to Kingston, Jamaica... I bit my tongue. This
family talk, among my in-laws, was mainly in Punjabi
and didn't really include me.

And, some months later, marry he did.

I remember it being said that my grandmother had gone
'into service' in some big house or other. It must have been
as kitchen maid because, when she dutifully opened the
back door to the baker's delivery boy, it was my grandfather.

In the eyes of his descendants he was a demanding husband.
Throughout her life, my grandmother devoted herself to
pleasing him, helping him on with overcoat and boots when
he left for a pre-lunch drink with pals at his local; having
the Sunday meal ready to the minute of his return.
Although suffering from a rheumaticky heart since her teens,
it was only when this reason for her living was suddenly taken
that she gave up, took to her bed and, nursed by her daughters,
was ready to join him.

Because I never met him, I hadn't grieved properly for my father's father who died in action in June 1918, a few months before the end of that war. Now, reading and re-reading the half-dozen letters from the front that have come into my possession, I sorrow over his poignant affectionate words to his eldest son, my father. I long to know him, what he was like; but there is no-one left to answer my questions. Was he conscripted into the army, a family man with four children and a new baby on the way? Could 'duty' ever have called him to volunteer to leave them? Only his pencilled notes remain, accepting of his lot, with words of cheer even when describing appalling trench conditions.

The new baby did not survive infancy.
I have only grandfather's words of pleasure at its birth, no record of his sadness at its passing

In recompense for his death in action his widow, my 'other' grandmother, was awarded by the local council, post-war, a secure job, so that she could bring up her four surviving children. On her knees, fingers bleeding from the coarse lye soap, she earned her pittance with brush and bucket scrubbing floors in
the neighbourhood school.

I barely communicated with my father while he lived:
Mum was the importance in our daily lives. It was
war-time when I was young, and he went early to work,
went fire-watching during the night, or to the pub
with his mates; while mum saw us to school, and in
the blackout walked us down dark lanes to unlit buses
for our weekly tap-dancing class.
Dad wasn't articulate like his father whose precious
letters, kept from World War I, say over and again,

*I am pleased to hear that you are getting on
very nice at school. Take care of your brother and sisters.
Look after your Mum and come straight home from school
in case there are errands to run. Wishing you all a
loving goodnight, your affectionate father.* And then
follow rows of kisses for his *dearest Bertie, Rosie,
Annie, Alfie and your Mum.*

Echoes of such feelings came once only - in the
single letter my father wrote me when India and Pakistan
first made war and I was in Delhi. He, a poor man, pledged
the fares to bring me and my children home if needed.

I wish I could have told him I had come to love him.

There were rats, rats as big as blooming cats
goes the old song.
Grandfather Harris wrote from the front:
the rats are as big as puppie dogs and the fleas
are as big as black beetles and you cannot
get rid of them; we can't get a wink of sleep.
So similar, and thus so true! My grandfather
was killed when my father was just eleven.
My other grandad sang me all the
words of the popular song and I learned them
along with my nursery rhymes, thinking them fun.
Because these rats and mice were in the Quarter-
master's Store and not in the trenches, and we
were too young to know the real horrors of War.
I sang the jolly song to my children when they
were very small and sometimes we'd march
about in tune to it.

I mourn now and always will
the grandfather I never knew;
the family he came from too.
Their name is Harris. No chance
realistically of locating them.
Last I tried the web-site of Genes
reunited there were over 2,000
newly registered in just the one
month previously, and again
each month afterward. How few
of these Harrises could in any
possible way be mine?

A pearl-handled revolver in the linen cupboard was all
that remained of the former role my mother-in-law,
a tiny but strong woman, had held during the aftermath
of Partition. Before my arrival she had been plump.
Her daughters, I later heard, blamed the stress of a foreign
and awkward daughter-in-law for her constant weight loss,
not realising, till symptoms multiplied years afterward, that
she was one of the rare victims of Motor Neurone Disease.

Although working with humble clay, my father-in-law as a young man newly returned from study in Japan and having secured a good tenure in the employ of a maharajah, wore only silk turbans and kurtas and drove in the one other motor car in the state at that time besides his Highness'. Little trace of such glory remained when I entered their lives. When Partition loomed, the family found itself on the wrong side of the border, and made an early escape to India from new-formed Pakistan. Luckily handloom cottons became de rigeur and suited sardar-ji just as well as the silk. When times were hard, *my husband tells,* his mother had to dye his brown shoes black in order that he could attend school. Later, on reflection, my father-in-law sent his elder son back to fetch out, whatever the danger, his valuable collection of Japanese and Korean pottery. This was kept in two glass-fronted cupboards in the lounge and frequently brought forth for art-loving visitors to admire. When another crisis threatened as he grew older, Daddy-ji donated most of his collection to the Chandigarh museum. In the old days the works would have been carefully kept, and so, in a way, many were - not, as intended, for public viewing, *it was said,* but dispersed privately amongst the keepers.

I read that bakers were considered to be in reserved occupations in World War II. Perhaps it was the same in the Great War, and accounted for Grandad Nash being sent to India with the catering division of the 'Queen's Regiment'. An elderly surviving relative recalls it was bread he made - bread that was sent out as far as Mesopotamia to our troops fighting there. Certainly he had a good time of it, with 'boys' to help out with the boring basic routines.

He returned with a stack of postcards, some brass knick-knacks and an enduring love of curry which he required my grandmother to make for him once a week. It turned out a very anglicised version of the dish with apples and raisins in it, but that was perhaps the way the British out there liked it. After all, they are credited with inventing Mulligatawny Soup and the like.

Grandfather sprinkled his curry liberally with white pepper and ate it with gusto. It was made for him alone, and he took no hand in its preparation - being a baker and husband, and not a cook.

74 Swaby

I went back down my grandparent's street after 20 years. It hadn't altered much. The green space, just trees and grass when uncle had run around its square with steadying hand behind my first bicycle, had sprouted a children's playground, swings and such. I thought that a good idea. Young mothers with pushchairs were sitting chatting while their kiddies played. We'd had to walk a long way to the nearest park when I was small. The house looked much the same too - the privet hedge, the red-tiled path, the tiny oval ornamental patch where little ever grew. An old man was sweeping leaves at the entrance.
I said, *I used to stay here once; it was my grandparents' house.*
He didn't seem to hear - or want to. I walked on.
Then I thought, *I must see if the brass letter box is still as bright and sparkling as my grand-mother kept it.* I'd helped her polish sometimes with the can of Brasso or the Duraglit wadding.
I think I always liked the task of polishing brass even though the wadding made your fingers feel funny. (*I use tomato sauce to clean my ornaments now - I saw it on the telly*). Nan's solid shiny letter box had been replaced by a mucky-looking white-metal thing.

I think that shocked me more than anything.

Auntie Grace had her own flat just around the corner and the gardens almost backed on to each with perhaps a couple in between. I used to go there with her now and then. She'd clean and polish throughout, though the place never got dirty; I never knew her to live there. There was a celluloid doll in the wardrobe with mothballs in the hem of her crocheted skirt; and a green china dog on the mantelpiece. That dog gazes mournfully past me today from my dressing table. I'd remembered him as happy and smiling.

On the night that my sister was born on the sofa at 74, I was sent with uncle Jim to sleep round at Tranmere Road. I sat on his chest most of that long night saying over and again (he told me) *Are you awake, uncle?*

Yes, muffled and sleepy.

Then why are your eyes shut? and I'd prise the lids open with my chubby infant fingers. Which was alright, except that, out of work for months like many others at that time, he was to start a new job early next morning.

All night I shared cuddles between him and the big china dog.

Childhood Christmases at no. 74 were big co-operative occasions full of family traditions. The ladies did the cooking: the men washed up. What was amazing was that it all took place in a 'kitchen' hardly bigger than a cupboard - just a small passage between the cooker and kitchen sink on one side and the dresser with all the plates, cups and saucers on the other. How ever did they manage all the peeling, slicing and chopping necessary to feed all the family, aunts, uncles, cousins that turned up? My Nanny cooked the goose and chestnut stuffing. Mum and her sister, auntie Grace prepared the vegetables. Christmas pudding was stirred by all us grandchildren. Silver thruppennies were put inside and considered lucky to find, but were collected back for the next year, as they were rare and treasured even then. Grandad had made the Christmas cake slowly over weeks before. It was laced with sherry and the layers of royal icing were built up over those of marzipan and jam.

Dinner always coincided with the Royal Speech which we listened to solemnly on the radio. Tea was with trifle, mince pies and the cake; and up in the front room, to keep us going between these meals, was a table laden with fruit fresh and dried and all kinds of nuts. I don't know where we put it all, but we'd chase balloons and, to the strains of a wind-up gramaphone, dance: the biggest treat reckoned to be 'waltzing' carried on the feet of uncle George, the youngest of Nan's brood.

Auntie Grace would play the piano as we passed the parcel and dealt our fantastic forfeits. Uncle Joe once had to call, *Winkles and water-creeses*, up and down the street. We'd finish always with games of housey-housey, and then we children would be packed away, four in the high back-bedroom bed with its rose-trimmed 'po' shoved underneath. And the grown-ups would sit up all night playing card games.

The "other side" liked nothing better than a knees-up. We'd walk from the sherry and pass-the-parcel to a crowded smoky room on the other side of the railway line, full of lively, noisy relatives, some of whom we knew. A barrel of beer stood in a corner of the front room, and the pint pots went round. Crisps, Pickled Onions and Ham. Here it was whisky mac I drank when I turned 16 and was considered old enough.

Both my dad and my mum's sister could play the piano 'by ear', but their styles were correspondingly different, to say the least. We'd all join in a sing-song, but the highlight of the evening was a quavering solo rendition of 'Burlington Bertie' by 'uncle' George Hartwell. Every year.

The two sides of our family hardly met, but my parents divided Christmas between them. When dad turned up one Christmas Day one year, late, drunk and obstreperous, Nan laid about him with a broom handle, drove him like a wild lion from the room.

He didn't come back to 74 again. But he never ceased to say, with admiration, that *the old lady was the best of the whole Nash bunch.*

Whenever we were parted by my long, though infrequent, visits 'home', my husband seemed to make new and close friendships with people I often found it hard to like. One of the stranger acquisitions was a couple, aunt and niece, who already had a reputation for hospitality of the sort most appreciated in Delhi then - the American kind.

Invited to a pre-Christmas party for our first meeting, I found their opulent bungalow buzzing with a lively festive crowd. An undercurrent of excitement, a frisson of expectation crackled in the atmosphere. Amidst the drinks and canapes, the bearer carried in a tray of chocolate fudge brownies, strangely timed, I thought, but perhaps a 'Yankee' custom. They were immensely popular and truly delicious - the best I ever tasted. They were served again at table - as dessert after a traditional Christmas turkey dinner. When second helpings were proposed I reached out, and was sharply told by a neighbour, to my discomfort and incomprehension, that I *should not overdo it*. My husband, who had drunk well of the freely flowing PX liquor, disappeared while our taxi was called, to throw up his lovely dinner and fudge brownies before leaving, and thereafter suffered no more; while only I, later abed, heard with terror my heart pumping its way out of my chest, as bright lights from passing cars dazzled my eyes through leafed hedges, closed curtains and tightly shut eyelids.

The doctor, summoned from his bed to save me, took great delight in administering a sedative dose into my backside as retribution for being disturbed for what he saw as my indulgence in illicit substances.

Friendship with the ladies ended somewhat abruptly.

At a posh wedding in the Taj hotel, the party
took pride in serving rare, specially obtained
champagne. My husband asked for beer.
In response to the hurt feelings of the hosts
he agreed to try the champagne if it were served
up to him in a beer glass.
            I was the strongly supporting wife
when, beaming, he took our leave and we wove
our wavering way from the reception hall.

Auntie Grace lived at 74 Swaby while my grandparents
were alive. She seemed to do most of the housework, although
everyone chipped in on Saturdays when the family gathered
for high tea followed by the grown-ups playing cards in the
back room while we kids had the run of the house. My nan
had a string of amber beads in her bedside drawer, and knick-
knacks on the dressing table. In the back-bedroom three picture
angels protected little children from varying dangers while the
pendulum of the grandmother clock on the mantelpiece tock-
tocked the slow passing minutes. Beneath each side of the
tall brass beds were tucked rose-decorated china 'po's'.

A case of old books stood
in the passageway, but we'd mostly gravitate to the front room
where an organ would wheeze in one corner; but more often we'd
tinkle out the odd tune one-handed on auntie's piano against the
opposite wall. Above this hung a picture of the badge of grand-
father's regiment 'The Queen's'. A glass fronted cupboard with
mirrored shelves held a myriad of ornaments, china mostly: red
tulips and watering-cans to tend them with, little figurines, and
a small collection of brasses grandad brought back from India.
We'd take them down to play with, sitting on the floor beneath
the gaze of child aunts and uncles in their layered frocks and
pantaloons, peering benignly from huge carved gilt-plaster frames.
After my nan passed away, auntie had the house-clearance men in.

And everything disappeared, exchanged for new.

I was 11 or so when first I took out the sheet music from Auntie Grace's piano stool and laboriously picked out the notes Doh Mee Soh, Doh Mee Soh *(Give me Five Minutes More)* etc. single-handed on the keys. When my little sister copied me, as she often did, we quickly discovered that she had inherited my dad's and auntie's talents for 'playing by ear' and was soon rattling off tunes with both hands.

I was never able.

Ted's dead. That's what my auntie said to me when I phoned her nursing home to find out how she was. Ted was my cousin, born the same year as I was, and one of only three Nashes remaining to our branch. The eldest's in Australia and recently celebrated his 75th birthday with big family rejoicings. I kept thinking and saying he was 80, and Ted and I should go over and join in - Ted and me only 68, *but you never knew how long...* Didn't know what it was that took him. Perhaps he followed the Nash tradition and his heart failed, as did his dad's and his uncle's, and his grandfather's before that.

I bit my finger nails all my life; no-one else
in the family did it. My mother accepted it
as one of my habits and did not try to stop me.
When my grandson started on his I felt it created
a bond, a skip-a-generation kind of likeness.
My daughter's disapproval took an active form:
bribery and coercion brought temporary respites
but surreptitious nibbles persisted.
Yet even I felt startled when I found him
chomping on his toe nails!

Suraj

One of our kitchen 'boys', of indeterminate, mature
years, was an odd fellow and a good plain cook.
He could serve chappaties singly at a dinner party,
piping hot, although he had to run a hundred yards
each way between his black hole of a kitchen
and the front lounge.

Outdoors, he'd amaze the children by
covering his head with a greasy dishcloth and cawing
beneath it so that the crows would get excited and
dive-bomb him to release their fellow they thought
he held trapped.

Once I caught my mother-in-law with
his nose tweaked hard between her fingers in punishment
for some misdemeanour. He made no complaint. But when
I accused him of appropriating my personal kitchen knife,
he clamoured he was innocent, hurt and abused by me.

Desraj asked me whether I would like him to
call me memsahib or behn-ji. I had no objections
to his calling me sister. But because he asked...

How convenient, yet exotic,
to dine on a dish of curried flower
buds, plucked from our tree
overhanging the garden wall.

When first I coloured my greying hair red,
the pottery wives sent me leaves from
the henna hedge bounding our garden
that they harvested regularly.

The difference between me, a foreign wife who resisted Sikhism, not for what it was but because I am Agnostic, and a cousin's bride, my new-made friend and a Hindu-turned-Christian convert, was made clear to me one morning. A 'bhog', a regular form of celebratory devotion, had been arranged and Santosh and I planned a walk through the hills together while the rest of the family worshipped. But she was recalled from the gate and firmly told she must attend. An Indian '-in-law', she bowed to convention, and I was left to my own recalcitrant devices.

Within the year she had happily converted once again, this time to her husband's religion.

As far as I remember it was said of Auntie Olive that she was a convert to Catholicism. I don't know why - perhaps I could have asked - for she married my Uncle Alf, and certainly no-one in our family was Catholic. Cousin Jean was brought up as one, but we didn't talk about that either. We knew she went to a Catholic school and to Mass, but it didn't really mean anything. My mum was a Baptist, and we went to Sunday School when we were little, but none of us was ever baptized. Going to Christmas Midnight Mass sounded fun though, and special, and we always thought we might join them, but never made it.

Cousin Jean stayed close to the church in an unostentatious way. We didn't meet for years when I was in India and she moved after marriage to a village outside Bristol. She cared devotedly for her parents when they got old and sick, and for her husband's parents too. But when her turn came for quality time for herself, with her children grown and newly born grandchildren to dote on, Nature sprang a cruel surprise. Her hospital treatment she thought 'the best', and her first recovery from cancer surgery was hopefully long. True to herself, she dealt with her son's marital problems, visited and supported me in family exile, coped with recurrence of her cancer,

and died quietly, still trying to cheer others.

Pitaji, my husband's grandfather, followed the golden
rule: *After dinner rest a while; after supper walk a mile,*
circum-ambulating every evening the peak of his hill
summer residence. He successfully attained his hundredth
birthday, although he had not managed the walk in his
last year or so. His son, my father-in-law also reached a
venerable age. Rumours he had gained his century circulated,
but faded into '*next year*' as the birthdays approached.

Mending bridges after
my divorce, at last I sent a congratulatory card for his
hundred years; and just before he died...
Alas! I then found he had managed only 99 after all.

Father's sister, Auntie Rose was always kindly. Unable to bear children in days when the causes were not investigated, she compensated with a pug named Tony whom she doted on. In his later life, wheezy and waddling of gait, the family gave him the epithet 'Stinker' which probably hurt auntie more than anything. Uncle Arthur, having been a chauffeur famously for a while, *it was said*, with the DuMaurier family, was one of the first in the family to own a car. He'd come with auntie to take us long drives through winding Surrey lanes. We'd pile into his little car, sitting on laps in the days before heavy traffic and seat belts, and go off to admire spring flowers or autumn colours.

Uncle later took a job in Scotland and sadly bore auntie off to live far away. There she also found employment in a place, Cousin Jean says, of dubious safety, since all staff were required to always drink a glass of milk before starting work. *(That learnt but recently...)* Poor auntie, developing stomach pains and recommended by her doctor to drink a daily glass of Guiness to bolster her failing appetite, was ultimately found to have cancer of the pancreas, and came back to London where she died a painful death. Uncle, who had seemingly remained a devoted spouse, was given comfort by a Scottish widow. His take-over was finalised by his complete disappearance from our family's cognition.

I longed to get inside my ancestor's clothes, make of them real people, not just be content with ghosts and flat images in photos. I sought out my dad's cousin, still alive and a mere six years older than me. Memories he had, but they were jumbled, and came out in odd bits all over the place, not adding much to the greater picture. Great grandma came from a farm in Camberwell. Did that tie up with great grandad living in Hampstead? But that must have been Bertie's great grandfather, and my great-great. How did the Evanses end up in Wandsworth where, as labourers, they helped build Wardley Street, part of Lyddon Grove, and stabling for horses used in the locality? That was extensive work, but was it so badly paid, or could it be the size of the family that led them to take up totting on the side?

I remember going to Coventry with Rose, your dad's sister, says Bertie. It was to some relative's house - he can recall the layout of the parlour, but he can't remember the names. I'd had it from another source that Great Grandad Harris was thought to have married a Coventry girl.

There was a son I visited in Tooting. Big chap, an RSM in the Scots' Guards. No more details, but that must have been one of Grandfather's brothers. We have a photo we think shows that family: a large prosperous-looking man, a slight self- effacing wife, three young sons, a daughter and their dog. Which of the boys is Grandad? It would seem not the biggest, rather tough- looking one. - He surely became the Regimental Sergeant Major.

My mother grumbled at her brother when, returning
from a coach holiday with her and his wife, and
carrying most of their luggage across the park, he
insisted he could go no further without a rest. He sat
down on a bench. It was a hot day and the suitcases
were heavy. In her need for a cup of tea she railed
at the delay.
We none of us know our fate.
Mum never really recovered from his never
getting up again.

It was a bit of a laugh, the way that we returned 'home' to England after 20 years in Delhi. The cat travelled first and most prestigiously by BA; my daughter was sent next by Pan Am and I went to a back-street dealer to secure a ticket on Aeroflot, the only airline then to accept rupees in payment and not to adhere to India's punishing travel restrictions.

I quoted my ex-husband's name as guarantor.
They knew him well.

My mother attended a luncheon club in the years, widowed
and with grown children, she lived alone. She had enjoyed,
besides good hot meals, the varied social activities that followed
them. She played cards and bingo, liked to dance, won prizes
for having the best legs, and was chosen for the role of the
Queen in some Jubilee celebration.

Then all changed. Her special friend
at the club died; her lady friend from next-door moved away;
her son's work re-located out of London, making his Thursday
drop-ins for breakfast no longer possible; my sister remarried,
and I - I visited Sweden and began spending increasing amounts
of time there. To top all that, the lunch club started to make cuts.
Instead of food being fresh-cooked on the premises it was brought
in from a central Council depot and was often salad-centred.
My mother didn't much care for salads.

We knew she lost some appetite for life,
but we didn't know she'd become anorexic until, her kidneys
failing, we went to stay in her house while visiting her in hospital.
The atmosphere of loneliness hung so heavy it was palpable,
and in the fridge a row of red garden tomatoes looked out at us,
untouched, accusingly.

PART II

Friends And Relations

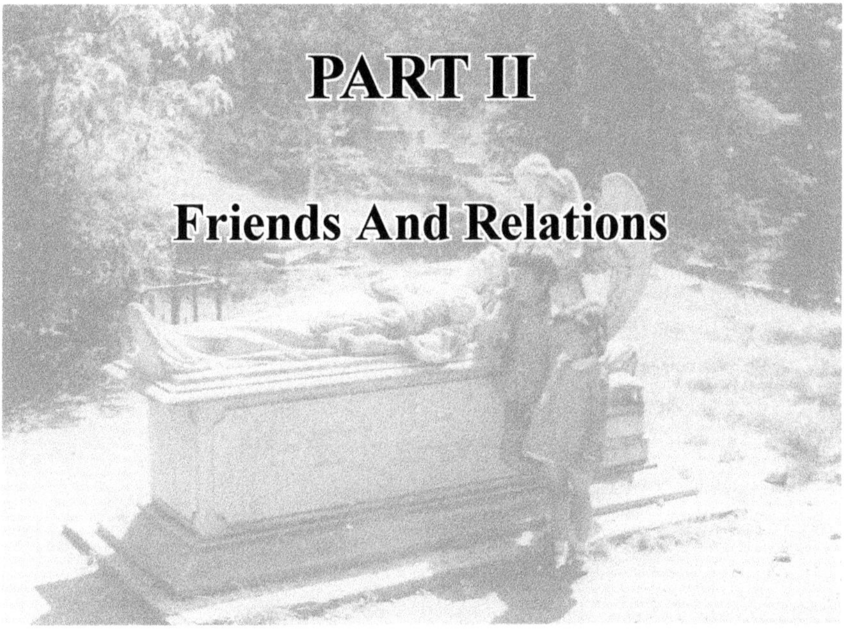

Four neat houses in a row on top of a hill: Middleton View was an apt address. The first was number one, of course, then three, five and seven. We lived at number three. It was a modern house with a proper upstairs bathroom. My best friend, whose home I visited, had an indoor bath, but their loo was out in their yard; while other folk lived in two-up, two-down cottages with slate-tiled back kitchens, and communal toilets in the backs between two housing rows. However did my father manage to find it?

I don't remember the move. Dad had made his way north alone from London in the Depression of the nineteen-thirties to take up engineering work in a tobacco factory and keep his wife and two daughters. That work did not last long; only a month after my third birthday World War II began and he was set to building aircraft in the Avro factory.

We were lucky living in a small town. Although a searchlight beamed a column of solid light some-where beyond the back of us, and a naval gun could be heard occasionally thudding in support, we suffered no air raids. A lone, lost German plane ditched its bombs over the other side of the valley; the motor of the only V2 rocket was heard to judder into silence above us early one Christmas morning before it swooped to explode elsewhere far off.

The biggest disruption to our lives was the blackout and, for us children, the limited choice of toys. Father was not often about, but he was not a service-man and there were summer days when my sister and I, dogging his footsteps round our little garden, learned to recite the names of his best-loved carnations: *Butterfly, Merlin and Mavis;* and *Ena Harkness*, his favourite deep red rose.

Coming from London to Manchester, our family accents were different from the northern ones surrounding us. I can't recall being teased for that in Infant School, but one of **their** general sayings irritated **me**. Whenever anyone complained of a thing being unfair, the usual laughing response was, *No, it's rabbits' wool!*

Even at that tender age, I
felt a need to explain that *fur* was the wrong way of pronouncing fair, so rendering the whole expression
invalid.

My dad had high hopes of my intelligence but I think I disappointed him. In Junior School I was always among the first three in class exam results, and Billy Dodson and I vied for top place more than once. But dad's sights were set on my progression to a good office job, and I left that to my sister who was infinitely better at it than I. My practicality he once summed up as: *Boil an egg? She can't even boil a kettle of water!* Actually that is one of the things I have perfected... with English eggs, that is. Swedish eggs react somewhat differently I've found, and my partner insists that only he may cook them.

Among the oddments Grandad brought back from his tour
of duty in India was a tiny brass man whose fist aloft must once
have held a spear, whose legs bowed outward once have sat upon
a horse. His turban was small, unornamented, his face pinched
and ugly; but I somehow 'took' to him, and was allowed to
keep him for my own.
Of a sudden I began to carry him around everywhere I went.
And so he was in my pocket when Margery Unsworth and I
visited the sandy patch across the field where upright wooden
sleepers formed a fence before the railway lines. We made a
castle there with turrets above and a passage dug from side to
side beneath. I placed the brass man under there in play. The
sound of engines whistling and shunting drew us to peer at them
through the planking. When I turned to collect the little man,
he had vanished from his tunnel. Nor was he ever found in the
search and destruction of the castle. Margery said she did not
take him.

Aged nine I lost him, at sixty-nine I still recall.

Going to school had its own hazards. Whenever cows were turned into the field before our house we were always anxious, peering at their under-sides, searching for a lone bull, jumping whenever a young bullock turned toward us. Once, on the steep sloped exit, holding hands and hurrying in fear of being late, one of us tripped and we all three fell. My sister grazed her leg, mother's tooth cut her lip, and I had a line of scratches down my nose. We limped back home; no school that day. Older, and independently, I was called out with other latecomers (all boys) before the whole school assembly to receive two strokes of Headmaster Garnett's cane. I didn't hold it against him. Every Christmas time he'd read out Dickens' *Christmas Carol* in daily installments; and he praised my reading-aloud abilities in the classroom.

Returning home was another matter. Alone, the weather caught me out twice. Crossing the field, in the hard winter of '45 a great snow-storm swirlingly blotted out the view and huge drifts made the landscape unfamiliar, the way impassable. Hopefully I kept fully to the right. If I could follow through to the corner, I would come to the banked lane behind which lay our little row of houses. Between the upright sleepers forming the railway's fence and a more-than-head -high wall of snow I found a narrow passage and came safely through. Another year some time before, in a dense and solid-seeming fog, I had blundered far out of my way in a panic until, a precious landmark, the familiar fence, loomed. With the same suddeness, the shadow of a non-fearsome stranger reared up, the only clear thing about him his voice, *Where're you headed, lass?* reassuring me that I was on the right track before he was swallowed in the blanketting mist. By that time I had my bearings and home was a short zig-zag away.

Mrs. Jacques' class was never popular. Were you ever made to sing Brahms' Cradle Song when you were only eight? The boys and I hated it. Those high notes! And when we could not reach them Mrs Jacques would turn to Winnie Heywood to show us how it should be done. She'd warble away at *'Home Sweet Home',* her voice swooping upwards, and we'd sit scowling.

One day, Mrs. Jacques smiled ingratiatingly at the class, *Hands up those who don't like singing,* she said. *Come along, you can tell me. There's no harm in it.* Hesitantly my hand crept up alongside four of the boys'.

Out to the front, barked deceitful Mrs. Jacques. *Stand in a row.* Miserably we obeyed. Striking a note on the piano, *Now sing,* she commanded. We writhed, but could not utter a sound. Another peremptory note, and quaveringly, tunelessly the boys joined in.

Outraged at her duplicity I remained defiantly silent. My voice would have been as gruff as theirs. At the end of the humiliation she let us back back to our seats without further comment.

Many of the children at my school wore clogs. I was fascinated by the process of repair - replacing the worn iron cleats on the wooden soles; the children waited while the shoe mender worked - rather like taking a horse to be shod. Most clogs were plain black with a buckle fastening, but one girl I knew had an ankle-strapped pair in dark green. I so much desired some like hers, and badgered my mother to buy me a pair. Eventually she gave way in part.
She had managed to get me some beautiful, memorable shoes even in war-time – a patent-leather pair in red, grey snakeskin ankle straps, and a white, summery pair for the church anniversary walk - so the clogs were a great compromise in style. They had wooden soles but instead of the ringing metal cleats there were corresponding dull hard-leather strips. The leather tops were not plain, but two-coloured, red and tan, with a T-strap fastening. Alas, they had none of the toughness of the other kids' well-weathered, long-lasting footwear.
The first time it snowed, they and my feet got wet and the red colour transferred itself to my socks.
Over time, feminine footwear progressed through the ubiquitous summer flip-flops to the dainty sequinned slippers and shoes so popular today. But long, long ago in the 1950's, my Indian boy-friend found for me leather thongs, then rare, in white and gold at Bata's in Ken High Street. And my feet fitted into them as if they had always known the way.

When I fell ill when I was only eight, Mum went out to buy me new pyjamas for Dr. Hemplin's home visit. Because supplies were limited, or maybe it was something to do with the coupons, they turned out to be boys' 'jarmies with very definite blue stripes. Scarlet Fever was the diagnosis, and an ambulance (*touch your toes, touch your nose, never go in one of those*) was sent for to convey me to the local isolation hospital. You could see out of the vehicle's dark windows but not in.

Hospital visitors were not allowed, and I'd never been away from my family before. They came once and waved from beyond the boundary wall - tiny figures in the pale sunshine. Yes, it was winter, because Christmas came while I was there. We were confined to our beds and fed only watery cocoa for the first week (*starve a fever*). When we got better we were allowed up. Because it was war-time staffing levels were low, and though we were young we were asked to help in small ways, taking food or drink to others. When I came to a toddler in a cot sitting on a potty, I was told I could take the receptacle away. The little one must have been sitting a long while, for when she jumped up the potty stuck to her - then fell off, emptying its contents over the sheet. I was no good substitute for Nurse.

As a special treat on Christmas morning the girl patients were to have a fancy hair ribbon tied. I vainly tried to explain that my mother **always** parted my hair in the middle and tied it with **two** bows; one would not be enough for me. Nurse told me impatiently that one would have to do and, zoop, my parting was made on the side. I didn't understand the probable paucity of ribbon, nor she my lack of worldly experience. She likely thought me a spoilt brat. For the occasion too, a huge fir tree had been set in the middle of the ward, and after its decoration, Sister herself came to place the fairy on the top. I was transfixed by its sparkle and, overcoming my usual shyness, sidled up to Sister and asked in an awed whisper if I could have the glittery doll for my own when the tree was taken down. She must have been amazed, but muttered a brief *yes* as she hurried to more pressing duties. I regarded this answer as a promise until sharply disabused of its likelihood by the nurse in whom I later confided my hopes.

As Christmas Day approached and I lay in my hospital ward, the dull atmosphere was stirred by a visiting clergyman who started to make the rounds of every bed. *That's Mr. Manby* I said to myself. He was the vicar of the church our school was affiliated to, and his daughter was in my class. I watched him as he exchanged a few words with each person and gave them a small present from his bag. When he came to me I looked up expectantly and told him that I knew Margaret. Alas, he looked embarrassed. He had only one present left, he said, and it was a book - a book for older boys. And so it was. Nevertheless, it was my present, and I took it and clutched it under the bedclothes that night, and dreamed of adventures to match the picture on the cover.

I had called out to my parents when they'd visited outside the hospital, asking my dad to make the dolls' house he had long promised me; but when they came to take me home, I had another request to make, an even more important one. It rushed out as soon as I saw them in the doorway. *Can I have long hair?* I had been nagging my mother for months, but she didn't want the effort of looking after it. Ringlets were what I wanted, and ringlets I did get. How could she refuse the dear daughter after such a separation?

Sadly my dolls' house never progressed beyond its outer shell, but I arranged the furniture I bought (costing 6d. and upwards from Woolworth's) in suitable groups, and imagined the rooms.

I was in the Oldham fever hospital the first and only time a buzz-bomb was sent over Manchester. People called it *Hitler's Christmas Present*, because it arrived in the early hours of that festive morning. I'd never heard one before, but I'd heard plenty about them from relatives living in London, so I recognised the stuttering engine sound right away. No-one else seemed awake, no nurse was in the ward. I hid my head beneath the covers as the engine died into eerie silence.

It was later said that, instead of falling direct, the rocket had soared in an arc and landed several miles away. For me there came no explosion.

My mother was ill on my 12th birthday. My diary records it, but I remember it too. I had to make my own cake. My first time, and I remember going over and over to her bedroom door and calling into the dimness for the next ingredient, the next instruction. We were still having to use powdered egg then, bright yellow in its tin, although the war was long ended. My results were not too good but, for me, baking still remains an elusive skill.

But the diary goes on to tell that my grandma, my father's mother, came to stay to look after my sister, my brother and me while my mum was in hospital. So there must have been something seriously wrong. But the diary has no details, and I gaze at the entry with surprise still, for I have no memory of anything further.

I remember only the birthday cake.

Nearly every week when we went to the library, I'd beg mother to take us by the slightly longer route, up through steep public gardens past the fountain whose central figure was a little boy that, standing naked, might have pissed had there been any water running through. But this was war-time, and ornamental fountains did not flow. Our mannekin's pedestal was elegant and free-standing, lofty to my small size. He stood quietly and gently amid the flower beds.

I've not been back to Middleton since, but my brother has, invited for some office function in nearby Manchester. He found and brought me a book of photos and stories of the old town. The whole was much larger than the part I knew. I turn the pages and there he is, not as a near copy of the mannekin pis as I remembered, but more akin to a Christ child, standing upright with hands outstretched. No wonder I loved to pass and spend time near that statue. Underneath, the caption reads: *Jubilee Park 1909. Unfortunately, the fountain disappeared without trace in the late 1950s (although it was rumoured to be in some councillor's garden!)*

For shame! How could this be? Was there no protest from the townspeople? I felt personally robbed, deprived; all of Middleton should have cried out.

When alone, Nanny would never turn the lights on. We'd arrive for our Saturday visit, and find her sitting quiet in the semi-gloom of firelight that filtered through the edge of doors on the big black kitchen 'range'. She'd say she didn't want to waste electricity. She'd heat a kettle on the range and, at times for her laundry, two solid little flat-irons, that were lifted off in turn with cloths around their hot handles. An enormous cast-iron frame supported Nanny's mangle outside the tiny scullery's door. On Mondays, sopping dolly-blued sheets were fed through its huge rollers while Auntie turned the handle.

Grandad emptied the tea-pot grouts in the drain close by the mangle when he made the morning tea - his sole, self-chosen daily chore. One day Auntie waited for the cup that never came. She found Grandad lying, his head near the mangle, still clutching the unemptied teapot. Nan took to the high brass bed they'd shared, her heart worn out with years of serving him, quietly, patiently.

Summer holidays took us yearly to Combe Martin, then a truly one-street village. Our boarding house, without electricity or running water (but candles and flower-patterned basins and ewers on Victorian wash-stands were an added excitement) stood next door to the famous, picturesque Tudor inn, *The Pack of Cards,* which was convenient for dad's and uncle Alf's evening drinks. Very much a mild and bitter man my dad once partook of the local cider to which he'd given little credit. That couldn't have been the time he heard about the mushrooms in the field above the house, for that day he rose with the dawn and returned with some, dew-speckled, and Mrs. Gubb had them cooked for his breakfast. No, he'd have been in no condition for, after he'd jocularly knocked back a few pints of cider, he expressed a guarded admiration for the brew since, in his own words, *I stood up to leave, and as I opened the door and the fresh air hit me, I fell flat on my face.*

In the school swimming pool changing rooms
I was mortified when friend Connie laughed
at my boobs - or rather my lack of them when
hers were well formed at just 13+ and mine
had barely begun to bud.

How could she know
that, in the days of Gina Lollobrigida and
Diana Dors, I would come to hold my own;
and how could I know that the strange *one
skin layer missing* she had often cited would
lead to kidney failure and a sudden early death
after she'd left school at 14, and I'd wheedled
one extra year in the Lower Sixth?

Amazing to find how exciting a sunset can
look upside down. I'd tip myself backwards
across the sill of our loo, situated half way
down the stairs outside the front door of our
flat in a post-war requisitioned house, to gaze
out delightedly. The bath was in the kitchen,
but we had sash windows: the only place
I've lived in that had them.

I love sash windows.

Watching the masses of people passing through London Bridge Station, I remembered the days when it was 'my' station, when I regularly took the train to work from Platform 1. I didn't feel small and insignificant then. Some fellow travellers were nodding acquaintances and some of the many porters were friends that, very occasionally, if you had just missed the train and they were having one, might invite you to share a cup of tea. The familiar Dartford line remains unforgettable: Deptford, Greenwich, Maze Hill (*peep out and upwards for a glimpse of the Observatory*), Westcombe Park, Charlton (*where Colin would get down for Siemens'*), Woolwich Dockyard, Woolwich Arsenal, (*here the soldiers would leave*), Plumstead. I can still recite on to the end of the line, but I got off at Plumstead Station, so that will do.

Student-nurse friends, Christa and I,
on first-time duty in Theatre, nervously
did non-sterile duties in the background
while the surgical team worked. On the
call for a basin to catch the contents of
a blocked gut, Christa took the necessary
steps forward; and I took two steps back.

Seconded to the local fever hospital for just two months with one other student as part of our 'general' nursing training, I felt rather out of place. The complex lay in an out-of-the-way situation, and I took along my recreational hobby of the time. I'd been given a small basic oil-colour set for my 21st birthday, and a colleague had lent me a booklet from her boyfriend - tasteful photos of very attractive nudes. I had visited the National Gallery many times, the first with a school outing, and I admired the figures painted there in the classical masterpieces. So I started on my first portrayal, placing the girl, whose picture ended at the knees, in a lake against a pretty mountain backdrop.

I concentrated on getting the correct reflections in the water, and trying to make a good copy of the lady, her head turned attractively away towards the scenery. The work progressed slowly - our nursing hours were long in those days and, with shifts, we often continued working until past eight o'clock at night.

A maid-service took care of our basic room cleaning, and fresh linen was brought, though we made up our beds ourselves, and put out the used. Home Sister over-looked all connected with our 'living in'. One day when I returned from the ward, my painting, almost complete, and the book from which I drew were both missing. Such were the mores of those times that I never queried their disappearance. Shyness and some kind of misplaced guilt prevented my asking who had removed them and why. No-one ever commented and I saw neither book nor painting again.

Squat and flat-footed, old Sister Gourley was the terror of Night Duty. For innumerable years she'd plodded her rounds. She had an eagle eye for small misdemeanours and she'd wipe the floor with any nurse who did not measure up. Woe betide those also, coming in late, returning to the nurses' home after some wild party or hot date. If Sister Gourley spotted you, you were in for a wigging or up before Matron. But she put the patients first and made sure you did too. The sick kiddies on Children's Ward were amazingly always glad to see her and would chattily respond to her surprisingly genial inquiries. When a new Night Superintendent was installed - bright, smart and youngish - attractive Miss de Wardt never elicited much response to her platitudinous overtures, and the children would turn away, sensing insincerity behind her smile.

Diagnosed in later life with ‘gallstones’,
the doctors’ solution is “taking out” the gallbladder.
Its removal is routine.
For me and mine, ‘Cholestystectomy’ sounds grander -
and much more frightening.

I have several gaps in my teeth now.
I think often of my little nan of whom,
toothless, it was said among the family,
she could crack walnuts in her bare gums.

My mother said
when she was in school
she had to make the choice
between geography and swimming
lessons. Though she remained vague about
the location of many countries,
it was she who made the long
journeys - to Australia
to visit her brother,
to New Zealand for my sister,
and to India where I lived for years.

The ship we sailed in must have been an old troop carrier. Travelling cheaply, we found our cabin fittings made of metal, as were the bathrooms, where the showers spat out salty water economically drawn from the ocean. Even so, there was a class lower than ours, for men only. In the forward hold bunks were suspended like hammocks, though their sleeping surfaces were flat and rigid and there was no space other than beneath them to place luggage. The passengers were relegated deck space in the bows amid the working sailors and the cables, and they would bring their food there in tin trays or 'thalis'. Our deck was just above, but we had a mess room besides, with tables and benches.

All classes were segregated; and though none of the 'hold' men came up to ours, I went down once by invitation and saw their communal quarters. More usually I would sneak, alone or with comrades, back into 'economy class', and even swim in their small pool. We should not have ventured: we were 'tween-deckers and not even on the passenger list! Yet here I met my husband-to-be.

I travelled out once more with the same French Company, to marry. This time I had a trunk below decks with, besides my clothes and odds and ends, my 'dowry'- a Wee Baby Belling electric oven and, because katoris had no handles, a saucepan and a large, lidded frying pan.

Hitting a small intimate bar in my exploration
of the forbidden bounds of the french ship, I
was held by the penetrating glance of a handsome
young Sikh. After an introductory sentence or
two he invited me to share his beer. *I haven't
enough money to buy one for you,* he said. When
I asked his name, *call me Minnie,* he replied.
'Twixt the look in his eyes and a rather a high-pitched
voice I was momentarily somewhat confused.

I had a near miss with a scorpion at the baoli when I went to wash clothes in the running spring water there. A small black fellow gazed back at me from the beating stone in full curled-tail glory, and was avoided. Although the amber is the less dangerous of the species, my encounter with one of these seemed the more evil in that it was hidden in the bed I had not long risen from, under the pillow where my infant son was sleeping. My mother-in-law disposed of it smartly with the kitchen tongs used for turning chappaties.

Pat says she can't write because there are too many mundane demands on her time. But she regularly changes all the linen on the household's two single beds every week; washes and dries and irons ... I will change my pillow cases as much or more than that, but my sheet will last me a couple of weeks or longer, and the duvet cover waits until it looks as if it needs to be changed, or until I tire of it.

In the winter cold of Northern India's unheated houses we were covered by cotton-wool filled quilts. People would travel with their bedding rolls, spreading them in trains at night, or in waiting rooms; and their resais could be used wherever they stayed. A few spares might be kept in cupboards for visitors who could not manage to bring their own. Once a year the rooh-pinjane-wallah came around, twanging his long carding bow. The resais, grown thin and hard would be emptied, the covers washed, then later the freshly carded, fluffed-up cotton would be replaced, and some low-cost tailor would be called to sew up and re-quilt them.

On an outing to the temples of Khajuraho, the whole family piled into my brother-in-law's Ambassador car. He drove, my father-in-law beside him. On the quilts ranged high and level in the back sat the rest of us - wife, mother, brother, his little daughter, Kiran, the ayah and me; comfortably, our legs tucked up. We spent the night in a Dak bungalow beside a rushing stream, where little else was to be found but rope-bound charpoi beds, a rough wooden table and chairs and an ancient chowkidhar watchman who cooked us chappaties and dhal.

Years afterwards, alone in the cold of a cheap hotel in Darjeeling, by the dim light of a 2-watt bulb I tucked the folds of a resai encased in easily washable muslin tight around me. It was hard to get warm and I snuggled far down. Next morning its streaked yellow-grey colours, conspicuous in the bright mountain light, determined me not to spend another night in that bed. But from the nicer, smarter, Government-run Guest House with its little electric fire, a hotwater bottle in the fresh-made bed, I unhappily contracted a vicious stomach bug!

When my marriage started to break up
only one of my husband's relatives showed
me any kindness - a cousin of my husband.
He, though only a second son, had taken
in hand the family land, and made it prosper
in the way of his father, who had received
a knighthood for similar expertise under
British rule.

The cousin and his lovely wife had a
family of beautiful, much-loved daughters,
but a son was seen as necessary to secure the
land tenure. They gave up after the birth of
the fourth girl.

His niece, daughter of the daughter
of mummy's sister, had married into India's
ruling family. Some dispute over earlier shares
in profits from the 'family land' was concocted,
and under pressure from officials and the 'law'
Minna had a heart attack and died.

Sadly my connection with the family
then ended.

My first Indian friends were Bengalis.
But I married a Punjabi. My husband's
later sweetheart was a young Bengali
maiden. Punjabis and Bengalis are not
supposed to get on.

But **they** certainly did!

Something of a black bitch herself,
Mitu insisted on introducing **hers**
to my dog Peter while I was away
because, *she said,* he showed homo-
sexual tendencies, having only the
big dog next door to play with.

Peter Puppy was given to us because
his owners had trouble controlling him.
He retained a tendency not to come
when he was called, and to run away
and explore when no-one was looking.
Once he was gone from us for more than
a week, and it could have been forever
if the gate to a courtyard had not been
left open, and if one of our pottery workers
had not just then been passing by, and saw
him tied up inside. In the end we had to
keep him tethered ourselves, and on his
lead for his twice daily walks. Even so
we could not prevent the consequences
of his desire to roam. He slipped his collar
one hot night when doors were left open,
and was found next morning on the boundary
with the neighbouring orchard, dead of his
wounds from a fight with one of the many
stray 'pi' dogs; *most likely over a bitch,*
it was said.

After all that.

We set off well enough, mother-in-law in her best salwar-kamiz, baby in his push-chair, Peter on his lead and I whimsically in a sari, for a semi-formal tea with two Anglo-Indian ladies, Miss Antonio and her niece, Kitty, familiar residents in the hill-station where Grandfather, Pita-ji, had his bungalow. On the quiet hill-top road I let Peter off his lead. As if on cue, a large group of monkeys arrived on the boundary wall ahead. *Woof* went Peter and shot off to give them what-for. Most of the troupe looked apprehensive, but the large dominant male, a fearsome creature, turned and bared his teeth at my small dog. Peter did not turn back when called. In alarm I rushed forward, and the whole tribe leapt away in fear down the mountainside. Gleefully wagging his tail, Peter took credit for the rout and jumped the wall in pursuit. What could I do but hitch up my sari and go after him?

Each time the dog drew near the monkey gang and I was far off, they would menace him with their long yellow fangs. Whenever I got close enough the group withdrew further down the steep hillside. The end was farcical. Both sides just came to a halt as though they found the chase no longer worth the effort. Then the monkeys moved off and a very dishevelled memsahib was left to scoop up her unrepentant pet and scramble back to make a notable entrance to the Antonio household.

As I viewed with detachment my son's 36 year
old rear rise as he bowed before the holy Granth
in honour at his grandfather's funeral ceremony,
I remembered bemusedly my reactions to the
sight of his two year old bottom waving in the air
in a similar situation. One can afford such
unconcern when time past becomes Old Age,
and this was now of his own free will. At that
far-off time I had been alarmed, dismayed and
angry at the hand that clamped his delicate neck,
pushing him down to kneel before the holy
book, and anger was the dominant emotion.
I profaned the sacred space in our Sikh home
and, trembling, seized and bore my baby off.
But that is how religion is handed on through
generations. Prayers are whispered into newborns'
ears, beliefs are instilled as customs, and emotions
engaged in the young before any reasoning can be
fostered in a growing mind.

Only survivor of three thrown from their nest in a storm,
Charlie mynah earned his name from the way he looked
performing his morning wake-up exercises. Before he left
his night perch in our bedroom he'd stretch, left wing up
and out, right leg out and down, then repeat the movements
on opposite sides. Next he'd crouch with both wings lifted
over his head, followed by a good shake of all-over feathers.
He looked a right 'charlie'. But then, eyes bright, he'd make
for the bed and, sometimes, with delicate beak movements,
give our faces a gentle clean up too.

Loved that bird! I kept him 'free',
not in a cage but, since I had had to bring him up, he would
often follow me around, and always slept indoors. Once at
dusk he had not returned and I anxiously searched the garden
for him amongst the mad cacophony of all the birds going
to roost. He was found at last over our back boundary fence
sitting forlornly 'lost' in a bush. His little pipe of recognition
as he scrambled and fluttered onto my outstretched hand was
rewarding and thrilling. Another time something must have
alarmed him, for he joined us outside as we tried to sleep in
a hot Delhi summer night and spent the entire time scrambling
onto the shoulder upper-most as I tossed and turned in the
oppressive heat.

Charlie tolerated a tiny cage for travel, but when
I bought a large one to keep him safe after he fell foul of a stray
cat, he became so depressed I had to let him out to walk around,
injured wing trailing till it healed and he could fly again. He
was sociable and liked his tipple, perching on the rim of your
beer or rum-and-coke glass and dipping in a dainty beak. Thus
on my brother-in-law's lawn in Kanpur, when the humans
adjoined indoors leaving him behind after pre-lunch drinks,
he was attacked by a marauding crow and hurtled after us,
squawking wildly.

In summer we took him up to the hills in the small cage. He patiently sat out the journey overnight and half a day more by train from Delhi to Simla. Once there he wanted to be free. He explored around our feet as we breakfasted on the terrace next morning and repulsed the advances of an inquisitive hill-mynah. However, hill houses are not like those on the plains. They have carpets, fat sofas and more upholstery than the stone-floored, cane-furnitured ones of the plains. It was clear our hostess would not welcome Charlie's natural additions to her decor. So when we set out for a long walk along the Mall to the bazaar, we shut Charlie into our tiled bathroom where he could move about without doing any damage. Alas! when we returned, the room's outer door stood wide open to the sunshine and there was no sign of our bird. We had not known to ask, and our hostess had not thought to inform us, that the jemadar came in to clean. When sent for, a tearful lady protested loudly that there had been no bird there when she came in.

No fault of hers. She had not been told anything of our pet, and if she had seen an ordinary-looking mynah perched inside, I'm sure she would have whooshed him out with her broom. Charlie, if swept outside, would not have been oriented to the place nor, from his Delhi home, have understood the concept of a hilly terrain.

For the rest of our stay I haunted that hillside, calling his name ever in vain hope. I never heard his greeting chirrup again.

How unexpectedly and hauntingly soft
was the skin of the baby buffalo that lay
beneath my feet on the floor of the jeep
taking him to be tied as bait for the tiger
our group hoped to see, yet never were
lucky to meet.

On a short visit to Jaisalmer we tried a mini camel-safari. Two young boys mounted us on their handsome, gaily-bedecked camel, Borah, and led us gently out of town to the former princely burial grounds where we rested on marble platforms beneath ceremonial chhattri domes. After being entertained by the youngsters with folk songs and stories of their lives while we waited for the spectacle of the desert sunset, we returned to our camel for the journey back.

Borah had entangled himself in the thorn bushes he'd been tethered to, as he foraged for a subsidiary meal, and was now very disgruntled. Disentangled, he refused to kneel to allow us to mount. The lads led him to the chhattri platform edge where we could slide into our places without his cooperation. Turning for home, he took a few paces before he was aware of our presence. He halted immediately, snorted, then to our dismay, reared and plunged like a rodeo pony in slow motion. Terrified, Margaret and I clung on. *Jump*, beseeched our equally scared camel boys.

A camel has long legs: the ground is far off. We hesitated... A camel also has a long neck and long teeth. Borah turned them towards us. *I'll go first*, I said hastily to Margaret from my front seat. I jumped, she followed; the sand was soft.

The four of us walked back to town,
Borah trailing sedately behind us.

A kerfuffle on the other side of the hedge: I looked over, into the luminous eyes of the calf next door. Doomed for his maleness, the Hindu family would not send him for slaughter, but to early exile, to take best use of his mother's milk. This was a brave and clever child: he'd returned home twice despite the efforts of the servant told to lose him. The lad had thus incurred the family wrath, and I'm afraid I added my insults to theirs, from a different viewpoint as he struggled to drag away the unfortunate animal. *Why do I continue to eat these creatures?* I wondered, and made an inner vow to try vegetarianism.

The eye of a chicken is somewhat manic at close quarters, but I came to love my brood. A dozen week-old chicks grew into ten white Leghorn hens and a lovely rooster with a gold-flecked 'mane'. Although they looked alike I could distinguish, and named most. There were, amongst, Lady, Penny, Tuppenny and Farthing ... and Tiny, who'd started as the smallest and weakest after the first that died early, but had since grown to be the largest when separated from the competition of the rest of the flock.

They laid us their eggs: one glorious day we had one from each. But after I stopped the anti-biotic addition to their water (provided on purchase of the birds, but was it really supposed to be used forever?) they became sick. And then I was trying to administer stronger doses as medicine direct

into their beaks. I'd croon *Cockie-Lock-a-Golden-Hair* to my rooster as I struggled to save him
who'd strutted boldly in protection of his flock.
No use. He slipped from my lap, dead.
I lost them all but two over a few days.
I never managed to become a vegetarian, but I
don't eat chicken.

Pippet, my little lizard, plucked from the garden, would sit on the back of my hand and snap up any passing fly. He never jumped away to escape, and that never ceased to amaze me.

I once went swimming with snakes. Apparently
fresh water snakes are not dangerous - unlike
the ferocious salty sea snake. In the streams of
our hilly summer place they appeared one year
only: green and gold, small and swift, and always
out of reach.

My darling little rat snake bit me just
the once - when I first picked him up.
But I had not been so foolish as to pick
up a poisonous snake, however small;
and Ratty would twine around my fingers,
more slender than the littlest of them.
I kept him in the cage made for Pippet.

On a picnic, coming across an itinerant snake charming group, I was allowed to hold the cobra, de-venomed, and a harmless sand boa with distinctive markings. When our pottery workers some time later triumphantly displayed the battered body of one of these latter, and the second only snake I'd ever seen on our premises, I could tell them that any such would not harm them. Knowing of my Ratty, they took it on trust *for the next time.*

Sent out of Delhi into the cool of the hills, there was little to do there but walk, and few places to walk to. Our chief destination was the local cemetery sheltering British graves from the early 1800's on. We would pass pleasant tree-shaded hours reading from headstones, memorials both poignant and entertaining. Our favourite by far stood out from the many crosses and urns. A gentle lady lay full length along her plot, her tiny infant beside her, cradled in one arm. An angel knelt protectively at their heads, with arching wings carved with great delicacy.

Somewhere along the years the statue became a symbol of motherhood for Hindus anxious for their fertility or needing a son. Since the custodians had long left and the cemetery was deserted, the women somewise began to chip away small pieces of the marble to wear as lucky talismans to help them conceive. And gradually the statue began to lose form, the mother and child to 'disappear'. A sadness lay in the fact that the memorial was dedicated to a lady-wife and her **unborn** child, carried off by cholera or some similar rife tropical disease that killed so many British in their prime.

They're gone now - as are the many glories and vainglories of the Empire.

India crept into my blood when I wasn't looking.
Only when I left it 'for good' did I realise how much
I was missing, how much a part of me it had become.
Earlier western visits were a delight of going 'home'
and holiday. But when that home became a reality
of money to be earned and life supported, then all
the oriental sounds and sights and warmth came back
to pulse against the walls of house and office.

Bound in by greyness, the dismal light
brightened mostly by the blue-white flickering of the
TV screen (once a luxury, now intrusive) the days
of light and pleasure are few and far between,
and to be hardly counted against hard-won pounds,
pence having become virtually worthless.

I would be back among pleasures remembered
- birds in multitudes in large gardens, dinners with
friends in grand houses, restaurant meals and cinema
visits easily afforded and taken for granted. With only
pigeons, sparrows and magpies about, can you guess
the excitement of sighting a solitary bluetit on my
rosebush?

When I entered a prestigious chain store
to sell dresses there, I did not regard it as
a step up in my varied career, but it was not
too lowly a sinking, I thought. Imagine my
amazed feelings of dismay when a store
manager told us one Tuesday morn that
the walls and skirting boards behind our
displays were not properly cleaned and we
ladies were to take a hand. Now, *hands
that do dishes* may stay *as soft as your face,*
but hands that wash walls and floor skirtings
would certainly seem at odds with the fine
silks and chiffons we were expected to sell.
Indignation expressed, Ann, our supervisor,
must have taken it up with management,
for the task was not performed by **her**
salesladies.

I promise: no more dead mice, I twinkled on being reprimanded for the little body discovered in a wardrobe wrapped in my hanky. I'd found the fresh corpse of a field-mouse on my way to work at the nursing home, and wanted to take it to show my grandson. My superior was not amused, but offered, magnanimously, a hasty burial in the grounds.

I held out, and took the little body home at the end of the day. My daughter was not upset, and toddler Jason was allowed a good look (but no touching) before we gave the tiny pretty one a decent funeral in our garden.

Where have they all vanished to? The admirable cleaners, always visible, proud of the gleaming environment of their wards, who would support and lend a hand at the lowliest tasks when needed; and the SENs, who might not require the book learning, but with their intelligence could spot and soothe away most problems. Their dexterity in handling both patients and equipment more than made up for any lack in fancy expressions. The student nurses, who learned patient care hands on, applying their textbook expertise. The Sisters who used experiences gained as staff nurses to become experts in the chosen world of their own field of excellence; who knew their ward and kept it SAFE.
So much has been lost to the political interference in the world of the professionals.

We are all worse off now.

In Sweden, Maud's mother's hearing aid fell into her glass of water and died. Maud said she was told that to get a replacement they would have to *return to the beginning* – ie. fill in an initial questionnaire and visit a hearing clinic: not easy for a frail bed-ridden lady in a nursing home. Attempts to borrow an interim device only produced the reply that the hospital was overstretched and *Demand exceeded supply.*

Lennart is a whizz with wires, machines and technology. He could even help with computer problems, though that was not his forte. Earlier employed to advise and help equip hearing clinics around the capital, he is now directed to close them down.

When the questions don't fit, my answers seem to match.
When the Asian boy, acting officiously, told me it was now
unlawful to feed the pigeons in Trafalgar Square, instead
of pointing out they already had mo1re than they could eat
in the sandwiches discarded by mainly overseas visitors,
I bridled and replied I was English and had fed birds there
since I was eight. (I have a photo at home to prove it – of an
excited child beaming; just one pigeon, attracted by the dried
peas sold then by traditional vendors, perched on an out-
stretched hand.) The boy said he was English too, and though
I watched his mind slow-tick, the question still amazed, *Are
you making racist remarks?* Anger blazed in me, and the
unthought-of *yes* shot out. Not true! How silly!

And long ago, when his wife suddenly asked through
the car window, *Are you in love with Sonny?* I stuttered feebly,
Yes. With a weak. *Sort of* added on because, unprepared, the
half-truth had flown from my lips. And when he later confronted
me accusingly with what she had told him, I could only yell,
Yes, sort of madly, sort of entirely; because at that time I was
cruelly and hopelessly besotted.

Auntie Dot sits among the living dead, waiting her
turn. All those she held dear have gone already - her
husband, brother, now even her stepson. My uncle's
second wife, she had no children of her own. Her
bodily needs are tended, but little can be done for
the pain that brought her to the nursing home bed.
It's a one-way ticket. She knows there's no getting
better. Her mind is still sharp. There is no-one left
near enough, in distance or in kindred, to regularly
visit. TV remains her only possible companion.
And so she sits.

PART III

Take This Hand

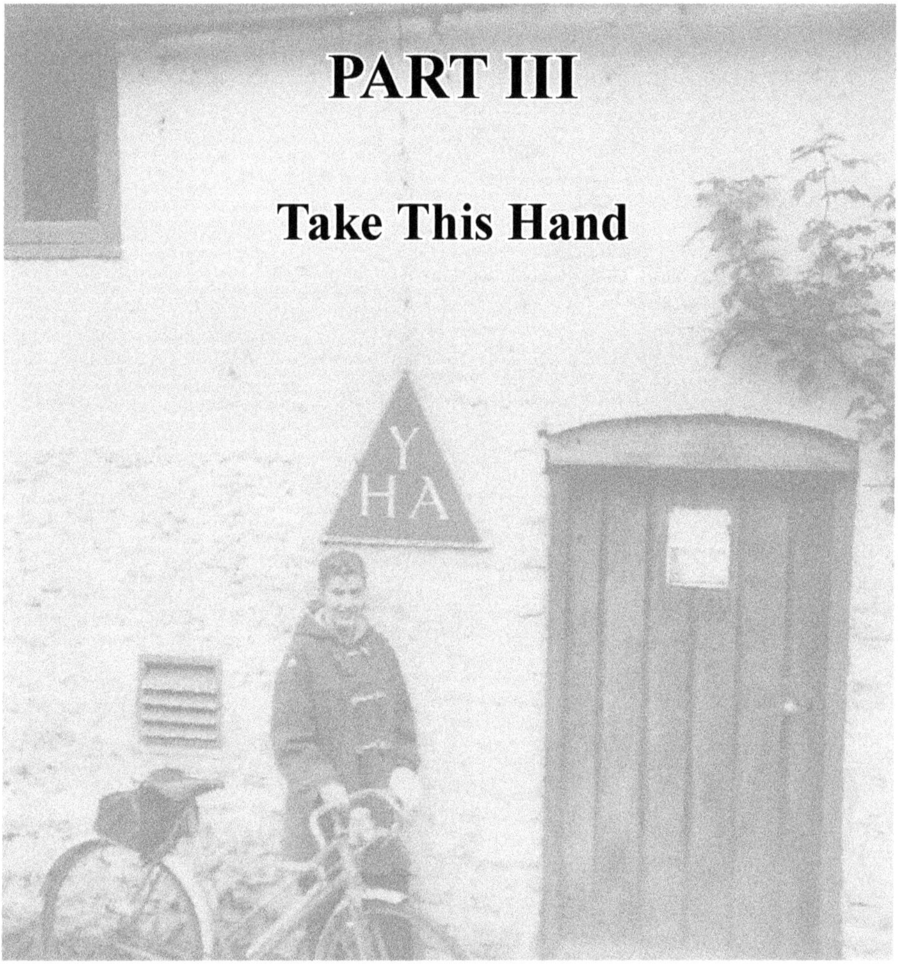

My cycling career started, aged eleven, when my uncle Jim ran behind me, his hand on the back of my saddle steadying my first wobbly efforts. He and auntie Grace had bought my first grown-up bike, a second-hand, sit-up-and-beg heavy-framed type named Daisy. She took me to school on swimming days when we had to get to the baths in Balham from our school in Streatham. My balance was always poor, and I was late learning to put my hand out to signal a turn. I realised I must learn when I misheard an affirmative to the question, *Have you put your hands out?* flung over my shoulder to my young sister and her friend, and a car whizzed by my front wheel as I started a right turn with no signal.

In my late-teens, I cycled down Oxford Street, looking into shop windows. Before I was twenty I rode to work in Woolwich Arsenal from my Wandsworth home, and a policeman who stopped me for some small traffic error at a vast empty crossing thought I was Italian (*he said*) because I was wearing shorts. When I cycled alone to Hastings, there were no motorways, and the highways weren't crowded. It was a long distance, so it took more time than I'd thought, and it became almost dark as I struggled up the South Downs' road before the descent to Pett. All other traffic was gone by then, and I was near tears as I pushed my bike, (almost new when bought from my sister and knighted after this marathon as Sir Ralph), yet still I reached the Youth Hostel before it closed admissions for the night. In those days you had to arrive walking or on two wheels, and you never had to book ahead.

Twice I've had rides on others' bikes - as a passenger, not pedalling a borrowed machine. The first time when I was nine, my cousin Ron, who later migrated to Australia, ferried my sister and myself on his crossbar, depositing us in turns by the roadside while collecting the other. In India, you may see families on bicycles, father pedalling, a young child on the crossbar and mother on the carrier behind holding the baby. So sat I decorously side-saddle when the man of my heart, with uncharacteristic abandon, whirled me on the carrier of his son's bike through the streets of his home colony. Later I owned a moped. Scant attention was paid to the Highway Code; the bullocks and their drivers were not expected to learn it. Nevertheless, there were parts of Delhi's Ring Road where in those days, traffic density being low, I could nip along at full throttle. However, I was riding slowly when a car came out of a hospital exit as I was preparing to turn into the entrance beyond. My speed was even more diminished when I hit it, but still I fell off on impact and the bike's front forks were bent. I remember a similar 'freezing' when, returning from school, I'd hit a loose pebble cycling into the home drive. On a collision course for the upstairs' baby's pram, I missed hitting it only because I petered out of speed and juddered to a halt just inches short.

I've never had a car, never tried to drive one. But then, I can't pat my head and rub my tummy at the same time - so I've always doubted my capability to co-ordinate clutch and brakes and gears, or whatever...

It was already past 4pm and dark when I ventured out to shop, carrying a plastic bag of bottles to put in the recycling bank on the way. Pitch black shadows, with the streetlamps gleaming sullenly on the snow, I avoided the car-park, a sea of ice; but my alternative path led to a similarly slippery slope. One step was enough to tell me it was unwise to proceed. Turning back, I felt no sensation of falling, just found myself on the ground, the glassware beside me, the fingers of the hand that had held the bag opening slowly not to close, and blood welling sinisterly in the palm.

I tied a hanky round my bleeding hand, but sat on
in the snow, looking in horror at the lax fingers.
Ladies who had come to collect their offspring from
the day nursery nearby came and stood. Looking up
at their concerned faces, *I think I need some help*,
I said.

Recent praise of Welsh Male Voice Choirs, justly
famous from the mining villages, tickled a memory.
How could such rich music pour from the throats
of men who worked in appalling conditions, where
lungs were often filled with coal dust? *My daddy
wishes he could sing,* I'd written, aged seven, when
he was bewailing the fact that he couldn't.
But how unfortunate that his unmusical croaks passed
down the generations - from him to me, from me to
my son - when my father's grandfather, who originated
in a kinder Welsh town, had never been down the pits.

In the sixties we'd flown, a proper family of four, by Iraqi Airlines to save money in affordable fares. In Baghdad we lost our plane to a party of French folk, delayed returning from holidays in China, who departed, each one clutching their copy of Mao's little Red Book, leaving us to wait in turn.

Offered a hotel to rest in, our planeload climbed into coaches, their doors locked for security - ours or Iraq's we were not certain. In searing heat we were ferried around the city in attempts to find places that would accommodate us. The hotel that finally agreed to accept such numbers looked so run-down that I asked if we could not return to the airport. No problem! Most of our group disembarked, to be returned in a couple of hours, sweating and dishevelled from beds in small, hot rooms, while our family had enjoyed the cool comfort of an air-conditioned airport with plenty of bench space to recline on in their absence.

We could not count the times we were served Macaroni Cheese on that journey. But it was a laugh then, and the Iraqi staff were simple people, and eager, if not able, to please us.

The kindly 'dagis' staff wrapped my hand in two tea-towels while we waited for medical help. The ambulance attendants insisted on carrying me on a stretcher for the short walk, but it was probably the only way to get patients slotted into the continental limousine-type affair.

A hand is the most complex of body parts. One hardly comprehends the full range of its movements until they are restricted. The young doctor in Casualty was not an expert. He opened the wrappings, gazed at the wound and PRODDED it! Then he re-wrapped it in a clean dressing and said I would have to go for treatment to the one hospital in Central Stockholm having a specialist hand department. I was conveyed there in a taxi summoned and paid for by the local hospital.

Along the way my doctor friend caught up with me. Thomas was concerned when told I would remain as I was overnight and be put on the operating list next day, since research he was involved with said speed was essential in the repair of damage to nervous tissue. But Government spending cuts in Sweden also meant that hand surgery was performed only in day-time working hours. He stayed and helped feed me my supper. The nurses put a plastic bag on the cut hand and told me to bathe and wash my hair.

Next day I was last on the morning's surgery list. Normal operational procedure was to block sensation by local anaesthetics into the nerve plexus at the shoulder, enabling the patient to be discharged home the same day; but I was relieved when the process did not succeed, and I had to be 'knocked out'. I think it would take a long while to stick together three cut tendons and four severed nerves.

I was proud of being English until
we helped the Yanks bomb Libya in
their attempts to oust Colonel Gadaffy.
I remember crouching unbelieving on
the carpet, while flames flared in Tripoli
On the tv. Kate Adie got a lot of flack
for telling how it was, but I admired
her for it - a last quirk of British pride
at her performance in a dangerous
situation. When I heard children in
Gadaffy's household had been killed,
I wept for our injustice and the loss
of my naive beliefs in patriotism.

Can you recall that girl in the pink short-sleeved
jumper? She appeared on my television screen, so she
must have been on yours. She carried her schoolbooks
under her arm and looked boldly out at us on her way
to college with colleagues of both sexes. That was Iraq
before the first bomb-shattering war on Baghdad.
I took to her much as others have to the naked fleeing
Vietnamese child, and the lovely Afghani who gazed
mournfully from the cover of *National Geographic*.
Those two have been traced in their later adult lives,
but who else noticed my Iraqi student, one among
others eloquently protesting the proposed Yankee-led
aggression? Did she survive those attacks? Or did she
simply disappear beneath the Baghdad rubble?
And if she could have survived, did she complete her
education? What remained of a life that had started
so hopefully as any student's might?

When I came round from surgery, a doctor's face floated into my woozy vision. *Would you like something for the pain?* he asked. I supposed I ought, nodded and, *bam*, a dose of morphine enough to fell a big strong Swede was administered, and a bed found for me in a general ward for the night.

Later on I couldn't pee... Now, if he had just asked *if* I had any pain!

My hand and forearm were encased in plaster, and cute little rubber bands were attached to my fingernails and at the wrist. A leaflet explained the exercises I was supposed to do, and appointments with the physiotherapist were to begin after the weekend. Stina guided me, but eventually became alarmed when I failed to extend my fingers against the pull of the thin rubber bands.

The doctor removed the plaster with gentle fingers. *Please give me back my hand*, I begged silently, *for I am a potter.* Her eyes were kind. Uncovered, the hand and forearm were stiff and bent like a dried-out tree branch, the fingers curved toward the palm.

Stina said, *work, work hard and exercise.* Yvonne made little splints to stretch the wrist and fingers and provided some games, and a loom on which I wove a long narrow runner in blue and white linen.

A senior doctor said, *Don't expect your hand to return to normal again.* Yet I would wake up nights, dreaming that all tenseness was released and I could move my fingers as before.

The epithet, 'Madame Germ' ought not to have
been awarded to one of Iraq's loyal professors.
The good lady did not herself release the results
of her research upon an innocent public. It takes
a politician to behave like that. No, I would award
the title to Mrs. Thatcher for her good work in
making our hospitals unsafe. Totally inexperienced
in medicine she sent like-qualified 'Supermarket'
inspectors to assess and decide the staffing of our
wards. On their recommendation, levels were reduced,
and that vital commodity, the ward 'domestic' was
replaced by privatised, visiting cleaners, so paving
the way for the spread of infections, including our
latest hospital hazard, *MRSA*.
Before, constant spills, accidents were always cleared
immediately with dedicated concern by the permanent
domestic staff on duty alongside the nurses. Men of
significance in surgical history, Semmelweiss and
Lister, campaigned for cleanliness as essential to
saving life. Mrs. Thatcher's economics overturned
such sensibility, and endangered all who must undergo
treatment in our hospitals today.

TV again, and Iraq again...
'Cotton-tops' the American troops disparagingly
call the folk they have 'saved', and many are seen
on our screens, unable to communicate in our language,
showing their grief at broken homes, destroyed lives;
veiled women gesticulating futilely at these foreign
soldiers. But this program is different, a reminder of
the other world that existed: an educated, cultured
woman pharmacist and her doctor daughter, speak
to us in beautiful English; not a headscarf in sight,
even at their work. Mother plays her piano in their
still lovely home: a Beethoven piece – surprisingly
appropriate to us in a week devoted to his works on
Radio 3. Yet, having endured Saddam's State, the ladies
now feel forced to try to flee their homeland. His
targeted rages had not affected their working or social
lives, but now the unending, uncontrolled violence
randomly unleashed upon the populace by differing
factions renders such past lifestyle impossible and
leaves citizens in fear for their survival.
Statistics say one hundred and twenty Iraqi policemen
are being killed on average each month. In place of the
former two-year training period, new recruits are given
just two months. They have to be got onto the street
a.s.a.p., you see, in order that Iraq can be seen to
manage its own security; and to take over patrols so
that American troops' lives may be saved. They are
unable to contain the situation they created, and Iraqis
have little choice in the employment available.
They make soft targets for terrorists.

History will redeem me, insists Tony Blair
as he requires the services of one hundred and fifty
English policemen to ensure his safe passage between
Parliament and Number Ten Downing Street.

On a bright, frosty morning it felt good to walk. I strode along, beside Stockholm's blue sky-reflecting waters. The sun was warm, the shadows cold. I was snug in my winter clothes. In the sunshine I sweated slightly; between the fingers of my damaged hand the skin became moist.

Later the cycle of pain began. The hand grew red and swollen; it burned. Everything I touched felt sharp; to my fingers my hair was like barbed-wire. The condition is recognised, associated with nerve damage and phantom limbs. A new doctor tried blocking the nerve transmissions at the shoulder plexus. It did not work, and on request, he reluctantly transferred me to the pain department.

Dr. Palmquist tried a treatment where she applied a tourniquet and injected the lower arm with anaesthetic. It was painful, but afforded a few hours' relief from the obnoxious symptoms. At the second treatment the relief was marginally shorter; at the third attempt it lasted barely an hour. It was pointless to continue. I was also given capsaicin cream to apply as a counter irritant, and Thomas, newly returned from Beijing, tried acupuncture treatment, but nothing seemed to work on this broken nerve-link problem.

What was left? The hand was becoming difficult to live with. Apropos the acupuncture, Thomas was now researching its effect on different pain conditions. Words like allodynia and hyperalgesia were grand ways of saying excessive pain for little or no reason - in effect a syndrome: and he knew drugs had been tested.

When the war was over, but fighting still continued, the people of Faluja were asked to leave their homes while the town was cleansed of terrorists. In *our* homes their destroyed buildings were on view, showing the few possessions - precious pictures and photos tilted on crumbled walls, and beds and sofas hanging precariously.

From the viewpoint of a Yankee patrol we watched soldiers fire at fleeting shadows among the ruins. Suddenly a tight group of black-robed civilians appeared around a corner, approaching without caution in anxious haste. A trembling soldier's voice was heard calling something indecipherable over the radio, then, faint but distinct, asked, *Shall I take them out?* Chilling the distant reply: *Take them out.* The camera recorded the puff of dust in the wide street. Then - nothing! I think terrorists hide in the shadows. I don't think they walk in a group down the middle of their streets.

In Iraq it is women who wear black.

I'm Walla, says the little girl, looking into the camera.
Walla needs psychiatric help to deal with the trauma
of seeing neighbours and passers-by fall victim to the
violence surrounding them. But one half of Iraq's
psychiatrists have left since the beginning of the war.
There are not enough left to go round and, of those
remaining, how many will stay in the hell Iraq has
become? The West always manages to accommodate
valued professionals, and so, as conditions deteriorate,
those who could ameliorate them, doctors, pharmacists,
the trained staff, are leaving for their own and family
safety; and Walla, and others like her are left to self-
medicate over the chemists' counters on valium, prozac,
amitryptilline and other mind-altering drugs formerly
available on prescription only.

In Haditha, another little girl,
Eman Waleeda, just nine years old, is able to relate the
tale of her family's killing at a Patrol's hands, while her
only remaining close relative, her brother, younger by
one year, is too traumatised to speak.

Sheik Jamal al-Sudani, *blessings be upon him,*
collects unclaimed Iraqi dead from the Baghdad streets,
takes them weekly for burial. A mortician by profession,
he arranges and pays for the interment of the unknown
(and sometimes unrecognisable) corpses - shrouds, graves
and grave diggers, and transport to the cemetery in holy
Najaf, 100 miles away. So many bodies; how long will he
be able to support the costs? And, *what is the use of numbers?*
another asks, *when every Iraqi can say that a member of
his family or a close friend was killed...* While he can,
Sheik Jamal goes on burying the unknowable dead.

Back to Dr. Palmquist. Yes, there were two drugs in main use: an anti-epileptic and an anti-depressant: I could choose! Well, epilepsy was something I didn't want to do with, and depression was something nearly everyone experiences to some degree at some time; so I plumped for the tri-cyclic anti-depressant. The deeper meaning was in the 'tri-cyclic'. For pain syndromes you worked up gradually to a dose that was still well below that given for clinical depression. Almost immediately after starting the therapy I felt the creepings of relief. Within the first week the hand's swelling and redness began to subside.

There were side effects. Dryness of the mouth was easy to deal with; the other I experienced sparsely and with some amazed enjoyment. Waking in the night, on rare occasions I would hallucinate. The first time, I had to duck beneath the trunk of the tree growing through the wall as I made a mid-night trip to the bathroom. Another time I met my daughter in the hall when she was really asleep in bed. Once, spiders, large and platelike, swung toward me on their silken thread, and retreated in ellipse. On another night, in like fashion, flew little men, floating on arms outstretched, their bulbous staring eyes, curled beards and ringlets speaking of ancient Babylonian carvings. I was never afraid. The images always appeared bathed in red light, and although they seemed very real, they disappeared when I closed my eyes! They were unexpected, personal and, yes, precious.

Nine months passed before medication ceased, winding down slowly as it began. And in that time I came towards the acceptance of my one-and-a-half hands - the 'half' still stiff and at times dubbed affectionately my 'wooden hand'. Apart from a blip, when I spilled hot cooking oil on it and had to spend the whole night with it immersed in a bowl of ice, terrified at the extreme, unreal reaction the burning caused, I've managed most things in my daily life. And I can still throw a pot or two. That's the main thing.

There they sat - a studio audience of bright young things, twenty and thirty-something, being quizzed on their hopes and attitudes to political party leadership. To a 'man' they declared they had had enough of Tony. He should go - immediately! But they didn't care for Gordon. No, he was dull. And poor Sir Mingus - he was too old - *over the hill*, although he did have a few good points to make. *A leader most importantly should have 'charisma'* was their final decision. So, for the next British Prime Minister they plumped for David - youthful, bubbly and inexperienced and, when it came down to it, the man most like young Tony had been when first voted into power, and now the most hated. I thought, *Charisma! What have they learned?*

And I despaired.

There is blood on the crest of Hokusai's great wave, blood from the rising tide of slaughter in our oceans; but the Japanese are blind to it. They defy whale sanctuary, and when they cannot get international support for their hideous killing, they buy votes from small nations too poor to resist their bribes.

Japanese art and culture, the fine fabrics, paintings and pottery, their love for cherry blossom and Mount Fuji lying hump-backed on the horizon, are all to be admired. But the whale is one of the world's most magnificent creatures, supreme in his element. Why cannot the Japanese admire this natural beauty, belonging to us all, instead of continuing to reduce it to a mountain of blubber which, in consuming, they come to resemble ... in my eyes...

Good fiction is the truest thing that there ever was,
says Arundhati Roy. And I feel that truth portrayed
in fiction often evokes as much sorrow as real life
accounts and news items. Reading the ocelot story
I was unable to prevent tears flowing. I seem always
to be crying for some cause or other, weeping because
I see no way for action that would lead to justice for
the downtrodden, the exploited or for Nature herself.
When I die, I have no desire for 'Heaven'.
I long to become an avenging spirit; not Mrs. Do-as-
you-would-be-Done-By, but a vengeful Mrs. Be-Done-
by-as-you-Did. Yet through the long aeons of humankind
would anything really change? So much effort is needed
by so many to make good; such few doing evil cause
destruction out of all proportion.
Perhaps eventually I would become weary
and long for the Nirvana I so fear now.

One day there'll be nothing left of individuals, no record
save that, once, a species known as the human race inhabited
this planet. All our strivings will leave just that mark
- we were here.

I find I'm such a mess of fears and depressions in my late years.
I am only grateful that when I was young and fair, I was
correspondingly joyful and unafraid; and that I can remember
that.

PART IV

And Then...

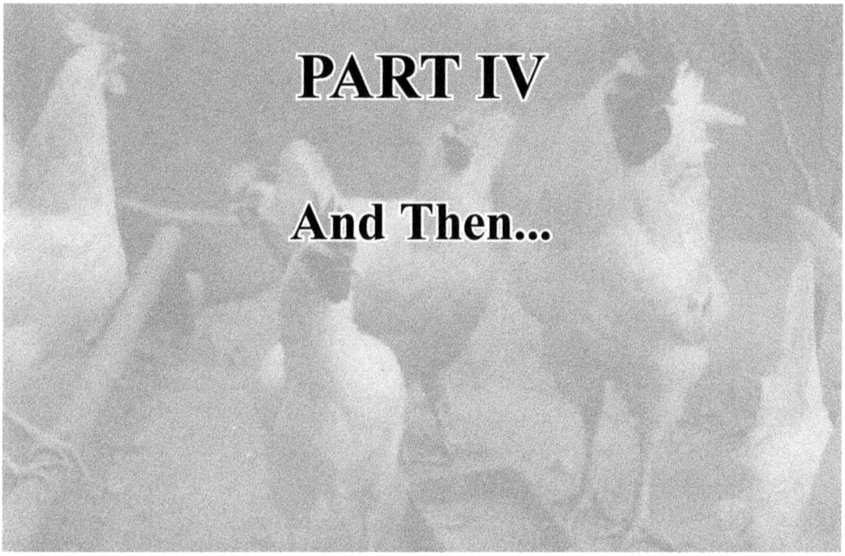

Monsanto's gone to India. They've a bright, smart office in Mumbai there, staffed by pretty young girls in bright, smart trouser suits, mouthing bright platitudes on the improvements brought about there. But in the country-side, those whose fields have not been bought up for development *(vast new townships with lots more bright, smart offices)*, in heavy debt to the sellers of seeds and other agricultural perquisites, take suicide as the way out of their misery and destitution, burn their desiccated bodies along with the stubble of their unproductive crops.

We met the 'Snake Man', Rom Whitaker, in the Madras Snake Park he had created. He was showing the reptiles to a small admiring public, and the largest python was draped becomingly around the neck of an exquisite, green-eyed blonde. People were allowed to touch the snake, and I stepped up to feel the silk of his skin and take his solid weight on my shoulders.
Cobras are less friendly and require greater care. They incubate their eggs, building large circular nests to do so. Conditions must be just right, and Rom, now on television, demonstrated. *I can talk loudly - snakes can't hear voices*, he told us. *And wearing this bright red shirt doesn't hurt either. Snakes are colour blind.* He is in Agumbe Agumbe where local folk still worship King Cobras, and where for the time being snakes are safe in their habitat. The jungle has 99% humidity - perfect snake heaven!

Elsewhere the old gods seem powerless, losing out to the modern world. Who will preserve the serpents of the greatest of all, Lord Shiva, whose sacred river is dammed, his people damned, and his temples drowned?

We had to put our black cat, Blue, to sleep because
the dog next door had died of rabies, and passed the
disease on to Beckie, our dog. Before she died she
and Blue were close. Afterwards, he'd slept and slept
unnaturally, hidden away up on the roof; but when it
came to the final sleep, Blue fought to stay alive.
It had to be done: cats' teeth and claws make it hard
to keep a pet and observe if the disease develops.
There were visitors and children to consider too.
But until this day, I see our Blue fighting, fighting
for survival as the vet had to put a final lethal injection
into his brave heart.

People seem to see my things as other than they are,
and dispose of them without asking. My father perhaps
could have been excused, finding my nicely roasted
brinjal cooling in the kitchen. Aubergines thus treated
do go black and limp, and the stalk could well resemble
an animal tail. At any rate that's how my father saw it
when he seized the par-cooked vegetable and flung it
through the backdoor. But what did my flat-mate make
of my lavender skirt, hung up in the wardrobe in an old
pair of tights to preserve its pleats? Out went that with
the rubbish as something unwholesome.
Did he think I keep hob-goblins or vampire bats?

Sausages can carry more weight than
one would think. When I whacked
away at a bundle from my freezer
for a reason I can't recollect, one
of them jumped up and hit me back.
Made quite a bruise!

In India I never met my Rikki Tikki Tavi, but did see a marauding mongoose that came at siesta time in the heat of the day. He killed every one of my day-old chicks on their first-week birthday. Only three were taken away, the rest of the dozen lay limp, with little blood or fallen feathers, but with a curious grey coil over each eye as if someone had placed a shell there in lieu of the ferryman's coin.

Later we bought another dozen chicks, this time already one week old and stronger. One died, and another, the runt, had to be kept separate for a while from her aggressive mates yet, despite being named Tiny, grew to be the largest of the flock. Most were named. Cocky-Lock and his 10 white hens: Lady, Penny, Farthing, Doucie and all, grew to maturity and, just one day, there were 10 fine eggs.

Woken to find moonlight running in liquid silver
across the bed, I searched for its magic path into
a darkened room. My partner, who'd just got up
to pee had left open the bedroom door, allowing
an alignment of the moon through kitchen window
and door, bedroom door and mirror behind the bed.
It had happened, could only happen, when the moon
was so positioned in its sky journeys that its beams
could strike the mirror at the rare angle and moment
they could be reflected across the bed. I called out
in awe, *Look did you see -?* And he broke in and said,
*It's just that blasted street lamp. That wretched orange
lamplight shines in every night.*
Orange! That said everything. He closed the door
on the bright silver river without noticing it at all,
and I said nothing more.

A large part of my childhood was during World War II. So my toys were rather limited, my dolls of the fixed, painted eye type and most obtained by my mother's sister, Auntie Grace, who worked for Triang Toys.
My first was Gracie-doll, named for auntie. Gracie had a cloth body and limbs, but her head was china; and when that broke she was replaced by Maureen who was of composite throughout. Topsy must have come next, for I remember her as old, with her eye-paint faded and her brown skin patchy, perhaps through lots of playing. She had had little woollen curls, but they were long worn away. I was very fond of her, even a little more than of Marie, whose painted brown hair, blue eyes and very red lips made a less pretty head. But I loved them all, and thought of them as my family.
Next came Sambo, a baby boy in a red knitted suit, very black, but with eyes that, though painted, seemed to shine. My last was a baby girl, rather delicate, with eyes that, oh joy, actually opened and closed, though they had no lashes. I found it hard to name her from my 3 favourite names at that time - Amanda, Sybil and Stella. My uncle wrote them on pieces of paper, and we pulled them in turn out of a hat: Stella, Sybil, Amanda. After all that, I decided I liked the 3 names too much to discard even one, and so the smallest doll bore them all, and in that order.
In such straitened times many dolls were hand-knitted at home from patterns in weekly magazines. I never owned a golliwog, though they featured in knitting and sewing patterns. Many children had them in the War-time and the days of Enid Blyton, and loved them, despite their being depicted the villains in some stories. Their image on jam pots was inviting and benign, and kids collected the associated golliwog badges.
So what was it made the BBC chiefs punish Carol Thatcher

(and bar us from this engaging personality) for mentioning hers, not even before tv audiences, but privately in their off-screen studios. I can't think she spoke without affection; but as with many celebrities, privacy is disallowed, and so-called political correctness is a bullying way for nonentities to denigrate and try to rule the famous. In such a climate what would be thought of my beloved Topsy and Sambo?

In times of so-called racism, how we see it through what we read is sometimes far more than our personal experiences. Newspapers are sometimes the bigger culprits in stirring racial tensions through their private vendettas with great folk. I don't suppose Prince Charles (who knows that Nanny Harris and Nanny Nash were my grandmothers, not my nursemaids) was alone in calling a friend Sooty (surely an affectionate nick-name of the Public Schoolboy type). If papers want to highlight nastiness, try Gorah, (Whitey) used in a derogatory way and applied to me when my only fault was to be married to and accompany my Indian husband on buses and into bazaars etc. from our New Delhi home.
And was Prince Harry hurtful to his friend in the use of *Paki* among comrades in a private video? OK, that epithet can be used unpleasantly by some, but **they** mostly go unpunished, and the tone and circumstances of name-calling should not be disregarded. Some insults can be dealt with in the manner of *Sticks and stones may break my bones but words can never hurt me,* or perhaps my half-Indian son got it right when he deflected stinging remarks from schoolmates by printing *I am a Paki Merk* across the front of his cycle helmet.

Brought down, brought low by age,
I who gazed up adoringly at my tall
lover, now find my eyes look into his
directly on his stooped frame. And
forty years on, my beautiful daughter,
who never grew higher than my eye-
brows, is now taller than me.

If I have just one recompense to set against
the woman who has now out-wived me doubly
through the mounting years, it is that she has
never hid her face in his black locks, nor
parted the long dark curtain of his hair to
gaze upon his beautiful youthful face.
But, ironically, I it was saved his endangered
life, for the two of us I thought, not another.

I learnt to type with both hands in school before I left, but not so well: so it is with pleasure, on a good day, when I see my fingers dance across the keyboard, lightly tapping, as if of their own volition, all the right keys. But, oh, the agony when, tired, keys are struck in the wrong order repeatedly, and there is the slow back and forth for corrections to be made... And then there's the sneaking worry in the back of the mind remembering Terry Pratchett, and his reported gobbldegook that left his fingers in the days of his established dementia.
At least, with computers, we no longer have to begin all over with a new sheet of paper in the typewriter.

Rabbits, don't you find, are just rabbits however cuddly pet ones might appear. But hares, once beloved of the goddess, remain special. Mostly solitary, one (at least) lives on the mound behind our flats. I've sought him out and startled him (and he me, for he sees me long before he leaps) away down the small hillside.

Tonight was different. Looking from our ninth floor window, I saw two hares side by side, companionably eating clover and dandelion stalks from the lawns below. People were about, and I hurried out to walk on the path nearby. Up went the long ears momentarily, but the hares fell again to grazing as I passed by, and they did not stop when I paused to watch, just gone past.

Glancing out the bedroom window in my absence, my partner
saw a wondrous sight: more than a dozen hares leaping,
rolling, cavorting together on the lawns below. It wasn't
evening; it wasn't dawn, but not quite mid-morning.
Is it in July then that the hares of Sweden turn into
Mad March Hares ?

When I was a child, the eggs we were lucky to get often had a blood speck (or more) in them, showing a chick had started to grow. Today's hens rarely see a rooster, and their eggs are unfertilised. Females of all species pass unused eggs, that is how life goes. So you might think sterile eggs would be seen as OK for vegetarians. Not for Nina though; my efforts to persuade her that using an egg in her cake-mix would not be killing could not change her life-time habits.

I often wish I'd managed to become a vegetarian. I made that wish when the calf next door tried vainly to cling to his mother and life... it is hard to eat animals whose eyes you have looked closely into. Apart from not eating chicken because I eat their eggs, and I formerly kept hens that I became fond of, I made no progress in giving up meat. But one thing I know: if I had an Udipi cook, I would eat nothing but his food; and the Udipis are the firmest of vegetarians.

In his first week at primary school, every day my little brother walked out of class and came home, even though the journey involved passing through several streets and crossing a main road.

So we shouldn't have been surprised that, when entrusted to my younger sister's and my care to see a kiddies' movie, on going to the boys' room and missing us he got himself home though it was a bus ride away. Babs and I scoured the cinema passages and then the streets anxiously wondering how to explain his loss to our mother, before reluctantly taking a bus home ourselves. But there he was, before us!

The school part had a good outcome though. New to the area, my mother, repeatedly returning my brother to class, made a long-lasting deep friendship with the young lass of a schoolteacher who herself at that time was a long way from home.

We used to play tennis together, my friend, Janette, and I; and go swimming and skating, when we were young and at school. On a holiday with my family, we even got lost together on a mountainside at dusk when we'd gone for a long walk inadvisedly late and, tired, tried to make a short cut across steep fields, hedged and nettle-protected.

But the time we didn't talk
together was later, when grown, and I found on her mantle-piece the telephone number of one I'd thought was my new boyfriend. I didn't meet him again, and she said never a word, even when asked about it.

A little mole, a tiny blemish, unnoticeable in
a place where the sun never shone for my
friend, Janette, killed her. When it was seen
and promptly investigated, it had already plunged
its tentacles deep; within the time allotted her
by her good surgeon, she was gone.
But nonetheless, in between, had found time
to nurture, even to dance and sing.

The Banstead/Epsom areas of Surrey were well-known for the plethora of lunatic asylums, the emphasis (mine) on *asylum* as a place of refuge:- the Banstead buildings, turretted and hidden in scrubland, were remindful of the fairy castle in The Sleeping Beauty; those in Epsom were set in extensive parkland. Gardening was allowed to inmates there, and I recall lines inscribed in my childhood autograph album:

Kiss of the sun for pardon,
Song of the birds for mirth;
One is nearer God s heart in a garden...

But what happened to all the hopeful landscapes? Modern politicians decided that the insane did not need space or beautiful surroundings; that gardening was exploitative, not helpful to them. Banstead hospital was turned into a prison, the Epsom units up-market housing. So the criminal and the affluent were catered for, and sterile, modern cell units were considered good enough for the insane.

Lord, I'd go crazy in one of those!

You think I don't yearn to believe in an afterlife? That I don't long to meet loved ones again? O how we have to live with our decisions, even if they weren't quite what we meant, or were misunderstood or misinterpreted. We have to live with them, and no chance ever of saying sorry to the departed.

When my mother's kidneys failed I'd begun to spend time with the 'love of my life', formerly estranged. My daughter thought I should not volunteer full responsibility for my mother's care if she were released from hospital; but share it with my brother and sister; and that is how the situation stood, never discussed or debated further in the family.

If love changes not where it alteration finds, certainly circumstances do, and true love should adapt. A mother is unique and irreplaceable, and my first duty should have been to her: but renewed romance was too strong. My not coming forward may have been seen as defection by the doctors. They did not say so, they asked nothing, but their interpretation was that my mother's life was not worth prolonging, and they let her go...

My loss forever.

They came and chopped down a tree
in the middle of our area, close to the
kiddy-park, where it made welcome summer
shade. It was a bright day, and the snow
had receded enough to allow access for
the dreadful, easy chain saw. One tree
had already gone, perhaps before the snow
had piled enough to prevent further taking.
Maybe the two were meant to be felled
together, two out of a small row of five.
They weren't in any way to disturb anyone's
view, or cause too great a shadow. They
were close-grown, but not too close, no
more than any others in our omrade. Their
sawdust lies like blood upon the melting snow.
In our warming climate, every tree is precious
Yet perhaps still more are meant to be taken.

Aaiyeee! Faluja, Faluja again.
A new set of images to torment.
Now the number of babies born
with deformities has sky-rocketed.
Many are visible and horrible,
but those of the heart or other
organs are more deadly.
Overworked doctors struggle
to care. At least the hospital
surroundings are bright and new.
Rubble from the houses that
were destroyed when Faluja
was first cleansed of terrorists
was bulldozed into the river.
How inane, crass, or deliberate
was that? For some citizens it
was the only source of drinking
water. The Americans don't accept
responsibility for the birth defects
but, there, they did build the new
hospital.

George Brown was a much undervalued leader. He was responsible for two actions I much admired: - providing pensioner bus passes – invaluable to old folk who for one reason or another could not drive, and finally, at long last, managing to pay off our World War II 'debt' to the Americans for their help in over-throwing the expanding Nazi regime. Did GW Bush ever contemplate recompensing Europe for its required contribution to the massacres in Iraq? And when one of his stated reasons for ridding that nation of Saddam was the bringing to them of 'Democracy', how could he justify congratulating Tony Blair for demonstrating his 'cojones' in overriding the wishes of the British people, who'd elected him democratically and who did NOT want the invasion of Iraq.

I suffer from mouth ulcers. I also had 'styes' on my eyelids when I was young. Gold was then the only 'cure'. Golden Eye Ointment was the most common application, but gave little relief. Auntie Grace supplied the other remedy - she would stroke the offending lesion with her wedding ring - an exercise in belief that the purity of the gold and the sanctity of the ring could 'charm' away the infection. It didn't work, but I submitted many times to the painful stroking to please my beloved aunt. My mother never tried her ring for such purposes. Then, it seemed very suddenly, - a new cream was available. Penicillin ointment appeared a miracle: the current stye disappeared with a speed that was astonishing, and I never endured another.

The case with mouth ulcers has evolved differently, alas, and they are not confined to the equivalent of an eyelid. They can affect the tongue, the gums, and all interior surfaces of the mouth and palate. I suffered over the years, when ulcers could cause agony with every mouthful of food, and the relief from usual remedies was minimal. When I tasted escargots for the first time, cooked deliciously by the mother of French friends, the gastronomic experience was marred by the presence of a large and furious ulcer in the most painful site for me - the labial frenula - the link between lower lip and gum.

Then a chemist recommended Adcortyl. Wonders! Minute amounts would provide relief for half a day; a night-time application bring about a much reduced lesion on waking. Two or three days' treatment and the monster would be gone. I kept a tube of this marvellous medicine with me on all travels. Recently, on attempting to replenish my supplies I was informed by the chemist that Adcortyl had been withdrawn. No-one could say why! Despair! Cruelty to sufferers, so unfair! Yet it seemed no explanation was deemed necessary to them from the unknown decision makers.

Mags said she did not want the book *Bad Blood* back
when I said I must remember to return it to her.
I don't know why, as children, we never took to my paternal
grandma. We didn't visit her as often as we did Mum's parents:
- every Saturday while Dad went to the pub with his brother
and their mates. I'd sit on the two little stairs in the hall and read
my way through old books kept in a dark cupboard there.
But though rarer, we also had good times with my cousin Jean,
Dad's brother's girl, who lived above Nanny H. and was loved
and looked after by her when Jean was little and her mother
worked. Jean and I played make-up games about characters
we found in books; I was once Sabrina to her Septima.
Such fanciful names, but the book title is unremembered.
Jean borrowed my book about Welsh sisters, Malys and Dilys,
and never returned it. But I too borrowed books that I always
meant to give back, and yet have the guilty pleasure of seeing
still on my shelves.

Auntie Min was always there on Saturdays,
in her black buttoned boots like those of my
grandad that my nan helped lace up and unlace
when he returned from his mid-day drink at his
'local'. I can't remember auntie saying much, but
we children somehow knew she could not claim
the same affection due to Nan, though we did
not know why. No-one told us of Carol, or talked
about her although, very much later, we learned
that Mum and her siblings knew and accepted
the daughter that Min had borne my grandfather
on his return from military service in India. Carol
had been taken into the family of an older Billings
brother, while spinster Minnie Caroline went out
as companion to ladies in Wimbledon. She had
first been inducted into the Nash household to
help her sister, Hart, look after her four children
while her husband was away. A fifth child was
born barely 5 months after Carol.
No wonder Auntie Min looked thin and bitter.
It must have been hard for both sisters.

It was a place of tranquility, perhaps because of its seclusion (it had been very difficult to find), perhaps because of the surrounding farmland, awaiting the plough, with last year's harvest remains still lying; but mostly because of the dark forest behind which formed a dramatic background to the small white-dotted plot of carefully tended war graves, a contrast to the normality of the rural scenery.

It felt right – a fitting resting place for my grandfather, a gentle man. Though he could never see it, it was a balm for us. A family-loving man, torn from wife and children in his early thirties to suffer the ghastly trench conditions, his scarce memorials are found in a few surviving letters:- gratitude for the gifts that reached him – a cake, some eggs, cigarettes; exhortions to his eldest son, my father, to *look after his mother, his younger siblings, and to be good, and diligent in his studies.* The final hope could not be lastingly achieved because my father was orphaned at the age of 11, and the family, impoverished, could not afford extended education and the certificates it would provide.

I lie in my bed
in a place narrow as a tomb space
and hardly dare twitch, accused of
taking his room in the bed that never
was big enough for the two of us.
There is a thud in my ear,
and an ache in my shoulder
which must be negated
against the roar of his
permanent back pain and the
constant two-hourly reawakening
in trips to the bathroom.
And so I cringe and whimper,
and cling to my edge of the bed
and sleep. Somehow *I* sleep.

Now am I the patient, unwilling, ungrateful
and in denial. So I refuse the treatment
(ongoing after surgery) meant to be 'insurance'
against cancer's return. But my brain shuts
down from what is painful. How else could
I have endured the discomfort and indignities
in discovering and mapping my 'invasive
growths'? And now, in my head, my excellent
surgeon has meticulously removed these
impurities, and I cannot bear the thought of
the remaining 'good' cells being blasted, and
I haven't the present strength to go through
more pain, more soreness or disability. There
are chores in house and garden that I must
attend, and travels I need undertake.
          I need the time.
I haven't the resilience of youth.

Ingram Content Group UK Ltd.
Milton Keynes UK
UKHW012052190423
420461UK00013B/252/J